PICTURE PERFECT

PICTURE
PERFECT

*An anthology of pœtry
and prose*

Compiled by

RICHARD DAVENPORT-HINES

Richard Davenport-H

Anthony Eyre
MOUNT ORLEANS PRESS

Published in Great Britain in 2023
by Anthony Eyre, Mount Orleans Press
23 High Street, Cricklade SN6 6AP
anthonyeyre.com

Compilation © Richard Davenport-Hines 2023

Richard Davenport-Hines has asserted his right to be
identified as the compiler of this work in accordance with
the Copyright, Designs and Patents Act 1988.

ISBN 978-1-912945-44-3

A CIP record for this book is available
from the British Library

Printed in Malta

Preface

This anthology celebrates the discriminate and life-enhancing use of words. Its spirit is contained in a remark of the Cambridge student of literature I. A. Richards: 'A decline in our sensitiveness and discrimination with words must be followed soon by a decline in the quality of our living also.' I rejoice in authors who choose the best words, put them in the right order, and create an immaculate sentence. My imagination is pictorial: I remember rooms better than faces, and landscapes more keenly than emotions. The poetry and prose in this selection create lively, inspiriting and sometimes unforgettable images in my mind. That is the only criterion for their inclusion. That is why the anthology is entitled *Picture Perfect*.

The poets who made a captive of me when I was young, Eliot, Auden, MacNeice and Stevens, are not included here. Their language, images and ideas have given me so much excitement that the process of selection and rejection would be unbearable. Besides, the copyright fees levied by their publishers are too high for me. Marianne Moore, Elizabeth Bishop and others would likewise leave me out-of-pocket. Some poems, notably John Donne's 'Satire III', Ivor Gurney's 'The Lock-Keeper', Charles Kingsley's 'A Rough Rhyme on a Rough Matter', Dante Gabriel Rossetti's 'Jenny', and Robert Southwell's 'A Vale of Teares', I have decided are too long for inclusion. I resolved, too, on finishing the making of this selection in January 2023, that I must not tamper with it afterwards. Subsequently I found the works of Wisława Szymborska and of Richard Tillinghast. It has been hard to quell the temptation to add 'A Great Man's House' by Szymborska, or 'A House in the Country' by Tillinghast; but I have done so.

Clare Addison, Nicholas Barber, Clare Bucknell, Jane Cooper, John Drury, Ursula Falconer, Grey Gowrie, Paul Quarrie, James

Stourton, and Andrew Wynn Owen gave me fine advice or quoted winning examples as I made my selection.

For years my friend Charity Charity delighted me with her sudden, apt quotations from both vernacular and classic authors. Before each Christmas she sent a booklet with choice tasters from her year's reading. After her death in 2021, so astounding and heart-wrenching for those who loved her, Patrick Hutton, her son, circulated a final pamphlet of her selections. His gift determined me to compile this selection, in which authors exult at beauty, and grieve at its loss. This is Charity's book. On the second anniversary of her death I dedicate it to her radiant memory.

Le Meygris, 19 June 2023

A Birthday

My heart is like a singing bird
    Whose nest is in a water'd shoot;
My heart is like an apple-tree
    Whose boughs are bent with thickset fruit;
My heart is like a rainbow shell
    That paddles in a halcyon sea;
My heart is gladder than all these
    Because my love is come to me.

Raise me a dais of silk and down;
    Hang it with vair and purple dyes;
Carve it in doves and pomegranates,
    And peacocks with a hundred eyes;
Work it in gold and silver grapes,
    In leaves and silver fleurs-de-lys;
Because the birthday of my life
    Is come, my love is come to me.

Christina Rossetti

Henry James said that this poem, which was written in 1909, 'performed the extraordinary feat of directing the contents of the poet's stomach straight at the object of his displeasure.' The target was Brooke's girlfriend Noël Olivier.

A Channel Passage

The damned ship lurched and slithered. Quiet and quick
      My cold gorge rose; the long sea rolled; I knew
I must think hard of something, or be sick;
      And could think hard of only one thing—*you*!
You, you alone could hold my fancy ever!
      And with you memories come, sharp pain, and dole.
Now there's a choice—heartache or tortured liver!
      A sea-sick body, or a you-sick soul!

Do I forget you? Retchings twist and tie me,
      Old meat, good meals, brown gobbets, up I throw.
Do I remember? Acrid return and slimy,
      The sobs and slobber of a last year's woe.
And still the sick ship rolls. 'Tis hard, I tell ye,
To choose 'twixt love and nausea, heart and belly.

Rupert Brooke

Advice

Inscribed on the porch of the temple of Delphi

Know yourself.
Nothing in excess.
Avoid a pledge [pledges lead to disastrous commitments]

To boys at a school prize-giving

Speak the truth.
Think of others.
Don't dawdle

Field Marshal Sir William Robertson

To pupils at Cheltenham College

Fly high.
Go straight.
Stick together to the end.

Reginald Waterfield

From a music master at Harrow School

Smile on the dung, as Mozart did.

to Edward Meyerstein

For politics and business in the Middle East

Always keep the initiative.
Always exploit the inevitable.
Always keep in with the 'outs'.
Never stand between a dog and a lamp-post.
> *Stewart Perowne, District Commissioner in*
> *Galilee and embassy Counsellor in Baghdad.*

Afterwards

When the Present has latched its postern behind my tremulous stay,
And the May month flaps its glad green leaves like wings,
Delicate-filmed as new-spun silk, will the neighbours say,
'He was a man who used to notice such things'?

If it be in the dusk when, like an eyelid's soundless blink,
The dewfall-hawk comes crossing the shades to alight
Upon the wind-warped upland thorn, a gazer may think,
'To him this must have been a familiar sight.'

If I pass during some nocturnal blackness, mothy and warm,
When the hedgehog travels furtively over the lawn,
One may say, 'He strove that such innocent creatures should come
    to no harm,
But he could do little for them; and now he is gone.'

If, when hearing that I have been stilled at last, they stand at the door,
Watching the full-starred heavens that winter sees,
Will this thought rise on those who will meet my face no more,
'He was one who had an eye for such mysteries'?

And will any say when my bell of quittance is heard in the gloom,
And a crossing breeze cuts a pause in its outrollings,
Till they rise again, as they were a new bell's boom,
'He hears it not now, but used to notice such things'?

Thomas Hardy

Two Irish labourers, Dennis Doolan and Patrick Redding, engaged on building the railway from Edinburgh to Glasgow, beat their overseer to death with pokers at Crosshill Cut in 1840. After their trial and capital sentence, 100,000 bystanders watched the procession of the condemned men on the four miles from Jail Square to the gallows erected on a hillock where they had committed their crime. Their execution was watched by Alexander Smith, then a boy aged ten or eleven. Smith left school soon afterwards to work in a Glasgow muslin factory. Later he became an urban poet. This extract from his prose work Dreamthorp *(1863).*

A Lark's Flight

The evening before the execution has arrived, and the reader has now to imagine the early May sunset falling pleasantly on the outskirts of the city. The houses looking out upon an open square or space, have little plots of garden-ground in their fronts, in which mahogany-coloured wall-flowers and mealy auriculas are growing. The side of this square, along which the City Road stretches northward, is occupied by a blind-asylum, a brick building, the bricks painted red and picked out with white, after the tidy English fashion, and a high white cemetery wall, over which peers the spire of the Gothic Cathedral; and beyond that, on the other side of the ravine, rising out of the populous city of the dead, a stone John Knox looks down on the Cathedral, a Bible clutched in his outstretched and menacing hand. On all this the May sunset is striking, dressing everything in its warm, pleasant pink, lingering in the tufts of foliage that nestle around the asylum, and dipping the building itself one half in light, one half in tender shade. This open space or square is an excellent place for the games of us boys, and "Prisoner's Base" is being carried out with as much earnestness as the business of life now by those of us who are left. The girls, too, have their games of a quiet kind, which we held in huge scorn and contempt. In two files, linked arm-in-arm, they alternately dance towards each other and then retire, singing the while, in their clear, girlish treble, verses, the meaning and pertinence of which time has worn away—

The Campsie Duke's a-riding, a-riding, a-riding,

being the oft-recurring "owercome," or refrain. All this is going on in the pleasant sunset light, when by the apparition of certain waggons coming up from the city, piled high with blocks and beams, and guarded by a dozen dragoons, on whose brazen helmets the sunset danced, every game is dismembered, and we are in a moment a mere mixed mob of boys and girls, flocking around to stare and wonder. Just at this place something went wrong with one of the waggon wheels, and the procession came to a stop. A crowd collected, and we heard some of the grown-up people say, that the scaffold was being carried out for the ceremony of to-morrow. Then, more intensely than ever, one realised the condition of the doomed men. We were at our happy games in the sunset, they were entering on their last night on earth. After hammering and delay the wheel was put to rights, the sunset died out, waggons and dragoons got into motion and disappeared; and all the night through, whether awake or asleep, I saw the torches burning, and heard the hammers clinking, and witnessed as clearly as if I had been an onlooker, the horrid structure rising, till it stood complete, with a huge cross-beam from which two empty halters hung, in the early morning light.

Next morning the whole city was in commotion. Whether the authorities were apprehensive that a rescue would be attempted, or were anxious merely to strike terror into the hundreds of wild Irishry engaged on the railway, I cannot say; in any case, there was a display of military force quite unusual. The carriage in which the criminals— Catholics both—and their attendant priests were seated, was guarded by soldiers with fixed bayonets; indeed, the whole regiment then lying in the city was massed in front and behind, with a cold, frightful glitter of steel. Besides the foot soldiers, there were dragoons, and two pieces of cannon; a whole little army, in fact. With a slenderer force battles have been won which have made a mark in history. What did the prisoners think of their strange importance, and of the tramp and hurly-burly all around? When the procession moved out of the city, it seemed to draw with it almost the entire population; and when once the country roads were reached, the crowds spread over the fields on either side, ruthlessly treading down the tender wheat braird. I got a glimpse of the doomed, blanched faces which had haunted me so long, at the turn of the road, where, for the first time, the black cross-beam with its empty halters first became visible to them. Both turned and regarded it with a long, steady look; that done, they again bent their heads attentively to the words of the clergyman. I suppose in that long, eager, fascinated gaze they practically died—that for them death had no additional bitterness. When the mound was reached on which the scaffold stood, there was immense confusion. Around it a wide space was kept clear by the military; the cannon were placed in position; out flashed the swords of the dragoons; beneath and around on every side was the crowd. Between two brass helmets I could see the scaffold clearly enough, and when in a little while the men, bareheaded and with their attendants, appeared upon it, the surging crowd became stiffened with fear and awe. And now it was that the incident so simple, so natural, so much in the ordinary course of things, and yet so frightful in its tragic suggestions, took place. Be it remembered that the season was early May, that the day was fine, that the wheat-fields were clothing themselves in the green of the young crop, and that around the scaffold, standing on a sunny mound, a wide space was kept clear. When the men appeared beneath the beam, each under his proper halter, there was a dead silence,—everyone was gazing too intently to whisper to his neighbour even. Just then, out of the grassy space at the foot of the scaffold, in the dead silence audible to all, a lark rose from the side of its nest, and went singing upward in its happy flight. O heaven! how did that song translate itself into dying ears? Did it bring, in one wild burning moment, father and mother, and poor Irish cabin, and prayers said at bed-time, and the smell of turf fires, and innocent sweethearting, and rising and setting suns? Did it—but the dragoon's horse has become restive, and his brass helmet bobs up and down and blots everything; and there is a sharp sound, and I feel the great crowd heave and swing, and hear it torn by a sharp shiver of pity, and the men whom I saw so near but a moment ago are at immeasurable distance, and have solved the great enigma,—and the lark has not yet finished his flight: you can see and hear him yonder in the fringe of a white May cloud.

Alexander Smith

A Painting by Winifred Nicholson

Sunlit green of a late summer hayfield
(The pikes all led and their faint circles faded)
Sheltered by abundant beech, goldening to autumn fire,
And beyond, soft English hills that close the view.
Some happy hand has gathered cistus, bergamot, scabious
From the untidy sheltered brick-walled border,
Taken a jug from the flower-room, and put them, just as they were,
(Giving them a little shake to free their plumage)
By the window, where a passing bee or butterfly may come.

'That is an old picture', my friend said;
And I, 'How like the real world you and I remember.'
—For those same peaceful fields of vanished summer
Were spread alike for ladies of the castle
And for the niece of the village schoolteacher.

Fields, it is true, in the aftermath are still green,
Beeches turn brown, country flowers in unheeded gardens grow.
It is something else, we said, that will not come again,
That leisure, that ease of heart unsevered from its roots;
The things we thought about, some sweetness in the air, nuance
Of educated English speech, libraries, country lanes;
Few cars; 'wireless' a cat's whisker and a piece of quartz
Boys fiddled with. But there was laughter,
Songs at the piano, the Golden Bough, the Spirit of Man;
Pressed flowers; how fondly we took civilisation for granted!

Kathleen Raine

Edith Joy Scovell published three volumes of poetry between 1944 and 1956. The precision of her poems, their sensory richness, the evocations of scenery, and her gift for drawing transcendent meanings from minute particulars are joyous. As she says in her poem 'A refugee',

> *All that I know of infinite is the intensity*
> *Of finite tenderness.*

Is it fanciful to see her as a metaphysical poet out of time? She was a graduate of Somerville College, Oxford, married a scholar of invasive species, and is described in the England and Wales labour register of 1939 as living at 98C Banbury Road, Oxford and engaged in 'unpaid domestic duties.' Later she lived at 61 Park Town, Oxford, performing the same duties and resolute in avoiding public postures.

A Present of Sea Shells

The shells are elaborate and curious
Like human thought, and yet not thoughts of ours.
A young boy searched them out on an island's shores
Where shells so perfect are not plentiful,
And in a carton, wrapped in cotton wool,
Sent them through air across the world to us,

Knowing that, settled far inland, we still
Love the sea's gifts, complex and beautiful.
This fact, this node of facts, in thought (like a shell
In the hand) I hold—the boy on the shore, the sun
On the wings of the mind-powered great machine homing in.
Time yields its patterned shells, none, none identical.

Waking in dark on the flat-lands of the night
To sadness, or space too vast, I light this light:
The boy designing our pleasure; and now, spread out
On a tray, the shells from their journeying. One is a dawn that pales,
One etched with finest fans on lapping scales,
One whorled; orange and green seem hand-strewn over it.

E. J. Scovell

August 1914

How still this quiet cornfield is to-night!
By an intenser glow the evening falls,
Bringing, not darkness, but a deeper light;
Among the stooks a partridge covey calls.
The windows glitter on the distant hill;
Beyond the hedge the sheep-bells in the fold
Stumble on sudden music and are still;
The forlorn pinewoods droop above the wold.
An endless quiet valley reaches out
Past the blue hills into the evening sky;
Over the stubble, cawing, goes a rout
Of rooks from harvest, flagging as they fly.
So beautiful it is, I never saw
So great a beauty on these English fields,
Touched by the twilight's coming into awe,
Ripe to the soul and rich with summer's yields.

❧

These homes, this valley spread below me here,
The rooks, the tilted stacks, the beasts in pen,
Have been the heartfelt things, past-speaking dear
To unknown generations of dead men,
Who, century after century, held these farms,
And, looking out to watch the changing sky,
Heard, as we hear, the rumours and alarms
Of war at hand and danger pressing nigh,
And knew, as we know, that the message meant
The breaking off of ties, the loss of friends,
Death, like a miser getting in his rent,
And no new stones laid where the trackway ends.
The harvest not yet won, the empty bin,

The friendly horses taken from the stalls,
The fallow on the hill not yet brought in,
The cracks unplastered in the leaking walls,
Yet heard the news, and went discouraged home,
And brooded by the fire with heavy mind,
With such dumb loving of the Berkshire loam
As breaks the dumb hearts of the English kind,
Then sadly rose and left the well-loved Downs,
And so by ship to sea, and knew no more
The fields of home, the byres, the market towns,
Nor the dear outline of the English shore,
But knew the misery of the soaking trench,
The freezing in the rigging, the despair
In the revolting second of the wrench
When the blind soul is flung upon the air,
And died (uncouthly, most) in foreign lands
For some idea but dimly understood
Of an English city never built by hands
Which love of England prompted and made good.

※

If there be any life beyond the grave,
It must be near the men and things we love,
Some power of quick suggestion how to save,
Touching the living soul as from above.
An influence from the Earth from those dead hearts
So passionate once, so deep, so truly kind,
That in the living child the spirit starts,
Feeling companioned still, not left behind.
Surely above these fields a spirit broods,
A sense of many watchers muttering near,
Of the lone Downland with the forlorn woods
Loved to the death, inestimably dear.

A muttering from beyond the veils of Death
From long-dead men, to whom this quiet scene
Came among blinding tears with the last breath,
The dying soldier's vision of his queen.
All the unspoken worship of those lives
Spent in forgotten wars at other calls
Glimmers upon these fields where evening drives
Beauty like breath, so gently darkness falls.
Darkness that makes the meadows holier still,
The elm-trees sadden in the hedge, a sigh
Moves in the beech-clump on the haunted hill,
The rising planets deepen in the sky,
And silence broods like spirit on the brae,
A glimmering moon begins, the moonlight runs
Over the grasses of the ancient way
Rutted this morning by the passing guns.

John Masefield

Leonard Barnes was awarded the Military Cross while serving with the King's Royal Rifle Corps in the war of 1914-18, attended University College, Oxford after demobilisation, and then farmed in South Africa. He became disgusted by British imperialism, wrote anti-colonial tracts, and in 1948 became head of Barnett House, an institute for social inquiry and progressive action based in Wellington Square, Oxford. His one volume of war poetry, Youth at Arms, *was published in 1933. I bought it after reading praise of it by Cyril Falls, an official historian of the Great War, sometime military correspondent of* The Times, *and for eight years Chichele Professor of Military History at All Souls, Oxford.*

Autumn

XXXI

...

Thrilling with triumph at a game well played
And sense of shrewd escape with no lost lives,
I laugh—and some titanic hammer drives
A red-hot chisel in my shoulder-blade,
Rips through, and out at the chest as swift as flame.
Plays from the mouth a gurgling fount of blood;
Then sinews all are loosed, and the limp frame
Sinks gasping and deflated in the mud.

XXXII

So comes at length rest from the flame and roar,
 Shell-tortured desolation and the breath
Of foul decay, all sights and sounds of war,
 From death and fear of death.

Here are white sheets and hands to still pain's smart,
 Voices of women and their touch, and ease
To read and dream, music to soothe the heart,
 And after turmoil peace.

XXXIII

Again this raging tiger Pain
Springs and mauls me; throbbing brain
And quivering limb cringe abjectly
From the pitiless claws themselves to free.
Wildly I fight, but the brute cat weighs
Too heavily, and swiftly slays
The antelope of my defence.

In odd detached indifference
One half my mind, like Mercury
In flight high over burning Troy,
Watches the agonized blaze
With passionless inquiring gaze.
The rest of me, the I that feels,
Enacts the scene and slow reveals,
One by one, pain's lustrous hues,
Vermilions rich and livid blues,
Flame-orange of fantastic sheen
With black of death and putrid green,
For the diversion and delight
Of this sole spectator's sight.

Only at times aware of the
Unmoved Olympian scrutiny
That sees but feels not, fiercely dumb
I writhe. Like quiet lightnings come
Flashes of ease; and then again
Dark roaring thunderclaps of pain.

The watcher's look grows keen, for see!
Agony's mad artillery
Has opened fire, and tears and splits
Resistance into flying bits.

The dreaded infantry follow fast—
Strange brutish whimperings, that at last
Capture the stronghold of my mind
And swarm upon my lips: spent, blind,
I melt in little piteous moan,
Like jackal's distant cry, foredone.
Then silence; and I conquered lie
In calm insensibility.

Leonard Barnes

Adomnán was born about 624 in Donegal, and was a kinsman of St Columba, whose hagiography he later wrote. He became the ninth abbot of Iona in 679, and was evidently a religious leader of rare wisdom, learning and culture. He wrote an account of Christian pilgrimages to holy places as well as Gaelic poetry, and became a saint to the Irish and Scots after his death in 704. He is commemorated in this poem by Tom French who was born in Kilkenny in 1966, raised in Tipperary, attended universities in Galway and Limerick, and lives in Meath. French is published by the Gallery Press, which has helped so many Irish poets to flourish.

After Adomnán

Because it seemed to sense that death was near
when it saw the old man pausing to rest
on the path where it had drawn milk to the monks,
like a person the horse began to mourn,

placing its head against its master's chest
until the old saint and his robe were drenched,
and servants intervened and did their best
to lead the creature back into the field.

But the saint implored that it not be touched—
'Those who have loved us and whom we have loved
must be permitted, at the very least,
to show each other what this life has meant.'

Thus, the old man whose last day was at hand
Held, until it had grieved its last, his friend.

Tom French

I was set this poem to learn as a schoolboy, and have never forgotten it. It was read by Samuel Brock at the memorial service in 2007 of his father Jonathan Brock QC, who had been at school with me. Shortly afterwards, while walking briskly down Holland Park Avenue reciting 'Already' aloud, I encountered a scowling policeman who seemed to think that anyone speaking poetry to themselves might be a threat to public order.

'Already' Said My Host

'Already' said my host. 'You have arrived already?
But by what route, what ingenious *raccourci*?
I half-expected you, it is true,
But I expected someone a little older,
Someone rather less arrogant and impulsive,
Someone a little embittered and despondent,
Someone, in short, not quite *you*.
And now you arrive by some unfair expedient,
Having neglected, no doubt, to pay proper attention to
　　the view:
You arrive a little dazed and flushed,
And you find me hardly ready to receive you, hardly able
　　to cope.
It was inconsiderate of you to die so suddenly,
Placing me in this ridiculous quandary.
I had predicted a great future for you,
A future without happiness or hope;
I had prepared a suitable mausoleum for your reception:
And now you arrive with a bundle of daffodils, a fox-
　　terrier,
And a still unfinished smile.
Really!

Michael Roberts

An August Midnight

A shaded lamp and a waving blind,
And the beat of a clock from a distant floor:
On this scene enter—winged, horned and spined—
A longlegs, a moth, and a dumbledore;
While 'mid my page there idly stands
A sleepy fly, that rubs its hands...

Thus meet we five, in this still place,
At this point of time, at this point in space.
—My guests besmear my new-penned line,
Or bang at the lamp and fall supine.
"God's humblest, they!" I muse. Yet why?
They know Earth-secrets that know not I.

Thomas Hardy

Ausonius was born in Aquitaine early in the fourth century of mixed Greek and Gaul descendent. He gained a fine education in grammar and rhetoric at Bordeaux and Toulouse. His former pupil, the emperor Gratian, appointed him as Praetorian Prefect of Gaul in 375 and a Consul of Rome in 379. He described the river Moselle in a long poem of which Sally Purcell rendered this version.

Ausonius, Mosella, 55 ff

This river has no secrets, we can look
through the smooth surface to its glassy depths.
As the soft hair opens clearly before us
when the winds are still and cannot hinder
eyes that see through space, here we look down
far into the inmost of hidden places,
see things deep-drowned as the stream slips by
and the movement of clear waters
shakes blue-green light over shapes below.
The sand is ridged and wrinkled by the current,
grasses bow and sway on the green floor;
the water weeds that grow there are shaken
by the driving waters, to hide and reveal again
the shiny pebbles, and gravel shows up the green moss.
Like this the shore of Caledonia seems
to the Britons, when the tide lays bare
green seaweed, red corals, and pale pearls, the seed of shells,
for man's delight, and natural necklaces
under the rich waves imitate our own.

Sally Purcell

Bermudas

Where the remote Bermudas ride
In th' Oceans bosome unespy'd,
From a small Boat, that row'd along,
The listning Winds receiv'd this Song.
      What should we do but sing his Praise
That led us through the watry Maze,
Unto an Isle so long unknown,
And yet far kinder than our own?
Where He the huge Sea-Monsters wracks,
That lift the Deep upon their Backs.
He lands us on a grassy Stage;
Safe from the Storms, and Prelat's rage.
He gave us this eternal Spring,
Which here enamells every thing;
And sends the Fowl's to us in care,
On daily Visits through the Air.
He hangs in shades the Orange bright,
Like golden Lamps in a green Night.
And does in the Pomgranates close,
Jewels more rich than Ormus show's.
He makes the Figs our mouths to meet;
And throws the Melons at our feet.
But Apples plants of such a price,
No Tree could ever bear them twice.
With Cedars, chosen by his hand,
From Lebanon, he stores the Land.
And makes the hollow Seas, that roar,
Proclaime the Ambergris on shoar.
He cast (of which we rather boast)
The Gospels Pearl upon our Coast.
And in these Rocks for us did frame
A Temple, where to sound his Name.

Oh let our Voice his Praise exalt,
Till it arrives at Heavens Vault:
Which thence (perhaps) rebounding, may
Echo beyond the Mexique Bay.
Thus sung they, in the English boat,
An holy and a chearful Note,
And all the way, to guide their Chime,
With falling Oars they kept the time.

Andrew Marvell

Breeches Church, Pollagh

*In order to estimate the size of the church and the number of bricks,
Canon Columb asked parishioners to kneel on the site...*
        Caitríona Devery, *The Story of Brickmaking in Pollagh*

He taught us more of faith in that half day
when he strode the plot to hammer pegs to mark
a nave for women and a nave for men
and, where they met, pulpit, altar, host.

The men threw off their topcoats then and dug,
sweating in their clothes, minding their tongues,
digging for the ground that could bear a church,
drills deep and wide enough for walls to sprout.

All that the tradesmen touched was true and plumb.
Their work was prayer. The pointed courses rose.
When the last brick was laid, the last slate nailed,
we faced where the manhood of our maker hung.

Tom French

I have used the original title of this poem, which was first published on 29 December 1900. It is generally known by its later title, 'The Darkling Thrush'.

By the Century's Deathbed

I leant upon a coppice gate
  When Frost was spectre-grey,
And Winter's dregs made desolate
  The weakening eye of day.
The tangled bine-stems scored the sky
  Like strings of broken lyres,
And all mankind that haunted nigh
  Had sought their household fires.

The land's sharp features seemed to be
  The Century's corpse outleant,
His crypt the cloudy canopy,
  The wind his death-lament.
The ancient pulse of germ and birth
  Was shrunken hard and dry,
And every spirit upon earth
  Seemed fervourless as I.

At once a voice arose among
  The bleak twigs overhead
In a full-hearted evensong
  Of joy illimited;
An aged thrush, frail, gaunt, and small,
  In blast-beruffled plume,
Had chosen thus to fling his soul
  Upon the growing gloom.

So little cause for carolings
    Of such ecstatic sound
Was written on terrestrial things
    Afar or nigh around,
That I could think there trembled through
    His happy good-night air
Some blessed Hope, whereof he knew
    And I was unaware.

Thomas Hardy

Cairo in 1930

The first sight of Cairo is not encouraging. Crowds of porters bay and scream; grey dust belches under the trams; clumsy blocks of flats with too-projecting balconies and narrow windows tower over the streets. It's all rather a bore—the thick boulevards, and trees white with sand, the high horns of cars and the incessant clamour of someone to sell something—a postcard, a necklace, a paper, himself—always to sell. There are public gardens of an average kind, with small flower-beds and large lavatories: there are straight streets, which imitate Paris in the kind and design of their shops—vaguely art nouveau, chiefly selling shoes and Kodaks. Here and there a square makes life a hell with rotary traffic or a violent whistle blows and blows from the police without effect. There are vast hotels and vast crowds of beastly Americans, quick passers in cruises from the *Franconia*, the *Esperia*, the *Adriatic*, the *Rotterdam*, I don't know what ships beside, who come and eat and defile the Pyramids, and remake their faces and go ....

I was quite alone before dinner on the lovely cul-de-sac which leads to the left of the Semiramis [hotel]. There was no-one there but an old beggar, half-asleep on a seat: it was rather dark, but one could just see the pyramids put a wedge into the sky. Underneath the stone embankment were a few crazy boats—a *felucca* or two; a house-boat; a launch, perished and ruinous on the grass, with broken windows; a steamer under tarpaulins with a red paddle-wheel. On one boat, a kind of house-boat, I saw a fire in a bowl, and around it three Arabs sitting, perfectly silent, quite quite motionless, their hands spread out to the fire like six oak-leaves, a red stream of light on their faces and a pattern of water faintly sounding against the dim garden on the side of the boat. It was as though all life was suspended but the Nile—everything held up in a basket between Time and night, with a motionless sunset waiting for the signal to go entirely away.

❧

In the afternoon we went to the Pyramids. The first thing about them is the disappointment. One starts out by car: over a cast iron bridge, through Gezireh, with a cloud of dust about one, past hideous, but hideous villas, all immense, all eccentrically Arabian, Gothic or Burmese-Palladian, towered, battlemented, above all immense, with the artificial green all around them of a well-watered sandy grass, inadequately large. Then the road goes into the country, past the fields of Slough, the water-meadows and munching incongruous camels in this ubiquitous countryside. There is a huge hotel after 6 miles, the Mena House, advertising a swimming bath—afterwards a steep curling hill with loitering English soldiers and kiosks to adorn it, and then, in a dusty sweep, a twirl of the car, the Great Pyramids, hemmed in with Fiat, Daimler, Minerva, Bugatti, Citroen Six, Ford, and a posse of donkeys. Round the back American women patrol in white breeches, and middle-aged businessmen take photographs of each other on a camel. There is a great deal of noise. Arabs clamour to be allowed to run up and down the pyramids in eight minutes. No obligation; all fun. Other people clamour to do other things. Nice donkey, sir: nice boy. I'll please you. No pay no pleased. Nice donkey. Nice donkey.

Alan Pryce-Jones

Card-Table

Always you were ready, revived by a good cup of tea,
To open the leaves of the folding table into a world
And from your rosewood box inlaid with ivory
Brought out the cards, the markers, or the board,
Switched off the flicker of the television screen
Where blacks and whites merge into indifferent grey
For an emblematic country where you, its queen,
Moved pawns and kings in errantry
Of ebony Spenserian knights and horses trapped in gold
Whose sovereigns held in check imperious heart and sword
And the invisible reaper delved his single spade
For lords of castle perilous and dark tower,
Your pitched court, your ever-embattled realm.

You liked to win; I too, though with less passion
Than you whose real world was all imagination
Untarnished by those ninety years that dimmed your sight and
   locked your fingers
While you and I wore out whole packs and sets of great ones
As tide of fortune ebbed and flowed, or skill prevailed
For you, by luck or extra-sensory perception favoured,
(Familiarly by your Scottish theologians named Old Nick),
But no sermons could restrain those wild ancestors of yours
From poetry, whisky, games of chance with cards or dams
Or their own brave blood-gilt persons ventured on the field
With no reprieve, honour and pride at stake
And hearts to mourn where knaves prevailed.
How well you would have played their reckless gamblers' game of
   life!
Now what a world of magic with that box is shut.

Kathleen Raine

Childhood

I

The old elmtrees flock round the tiled farmstead; their silver-bellied leaves dance in the wind. Beneath their shade, in the corner of the Green, is a pond. In winter it is full of water, green with weeds: in Spring a lily will open there.

The ducks waddle in the mud and sail in circles round the pond, or preen their feathers on the bank.

But in Summer the pond is dry, and its bed is glossy and baked by the sun, a beautiful soft colour like the skins of the moles they catch and crucify on the stable doors.

On the green the fowls pick grains, or chatter and fight. Their yellows, whites and browns, the metallic lustre of their darker feathers, and the crimson splash of their combs make an ever-changing pattern on the grass.

They drink with spasmodic upreaching necks by the side of the well.

Under the stones by the well live lizards curious to our eyes.

The path from the well leads to a garden door set in the high wall whereon grow plums and apricots. The door is deep and narrow and opens on to paths bordered with box-hedges; one path leads through the aromatic currant bushes, beneath the plum-trees, to the lawn where grows the wonder of our day-dreams, the monkey's puzzle-tree. On the other side of the lawn three fir-trees rise sharply to the sky, their dark shades homing a few birds.

Beyond is the orchard, and down its avenues of mould-smitten trees the path leads to the paddocks, with their mushrooms and fairy-rings, and to the flatlands that stretch to the girding hills.

2

The farm is distant from the high-road half a mile;

The child of the farm
does not realize it for several years;
He wanders through the orchard,
finds mushrooms in the paddock,
or beetles in the pond.

But one day he goes to the high-road,
sees carts and carriages pass,
and men go marketing.

A traction engine crashes into his vision
with flame and smoke,
and makes his eager soul retreat.

He turns away:
The huntsmen are galloping over the fields,
Their red coats and the swift whimpering hounds.

Sir Herbert Read

Amours de Voyage, by Arthur Hugh Clough, is another set-piece of school reading that has never left me. The tempers of the book—self-absorption, hesitancy, fitful arrogance, anxiety and timid love—are apt for adolescents in a hot-housed school. Clough was a former Fellow of Oriel College, Oxford who was present at both the Paris revolution of 1848 and the overthrow of the Roman republic in 1849. He used the latter experience to write a novel in verse form about English travellers who meet in Rome during the turbulence of 1849. This passage is from canto II, sections IX-XI. The last ten lines have been a personal plainsong throughout my life.

Claude to Eustace

It is most curious to see what a power a few calm words (in
Merely a brief proclamation) appear to possess on the people.
Order is perfect, and peace; the city is utterly tranquil;
And one cannot conceive that this easy and *nonchalant* crowd, that
Flows like a quiet stream through street and market-place, entering
Shady recesses and bays of church, *osteria*, and *caffè*,
Could in a moment be changed to a flood as of molten lava,
Boil into deadly wrath and wild homicidal delusion.
   Ah, 'tis an excellent race,—and even in old degradation,
Under a rule that enforces to flattery, lying, and cheating,
E'en under Pope and Priest, a nice and natural people.
Oh, could they but be allowed this chance of redemption!—but
  clearly
That is not likely to be. Meantime, notwithstanding all journals,
Honour for once to the tongue and the pen of the eloquent writer!
Honour to speech! and all honour to thee, thou noble Mazzini!

I am in love, meantime, you think; no doubt you would think so.
I am in love, you say; with those letters, of course, you would say so.
I am in love, you declare. I think not so; yet I grant you
It is a pleasure, indeed, to converse with this girl. Oh, rare gift,
Rare felicity, this! she can talk in a rational way, can
Speak upon subjects that really are matters of mind and of thinking,
Yet in perfection retain her simplicity; never, one moment,
Never, however you urge it, however you tempt her, consents to
Step from ideas and fancies and loving sensations to those vain
Conscious understandings that vex the minds of man-kind.
No, though she talk, it is music; her fingers desert not the keys; 'tis
Song, though you hear in the song the articulate vocables sounded,
Syllabled singly and sweetly the words of melodious meaning.
     I am in love, you say; I do not think so exactly.

There are two different kinds, I believe, of human attraction:
One which simply disturbs, unsettles, and makes you uneasy,
And another that poises, retains, and fixes and holds you.
I have no doubt, for myself, in giving my voice for the latter.
I do not wish to be moved, but growing where I was growing,
There more truly to grow, to live where as yet I had languished.
I do not like being moved: for the will is excited; and action
Is a most dangerous thing; I tremble for something factitious,
Some malpractice of heart and illegitimate process;
We are so prone to these things with our terrible notions of duty.

Arthur Hugh Clough

Closing Time

The outside of the Cathedral was ponderous, its walls solid and blank, heavy Spanish bodies. There was an earthy joviality in the faces of the prophets, saints, and Holy Family, good thick Spaniards all of them, crumbling on the pedestals, as the mystics do, half-way between matter and spirit. I passed under the Holy Family, a heavy door on its spring barked behind me, I stepped into a pit of momentary darkness, and then found myself treading a clear floor of stone in a trenchant reservoir of light.

The walls drove up sheer out of the mind's reach on either side to the wings of vaulting hushed above my head. High in the walls were stretched out the agonised stained windows breaking up the light into a sorrowful murmur of tones. The air was frozen wine, built up of the window colours, coloured ice that penetrated and knocked hard on the bones and picked out every hair on the body. That sharp nave was a dagger stab from a medieval heaven, a cut to the heart.

This Leon was so Spanish in spirit. Outside you had the heavy cocido walls—the beans, the fat, the spices, the gravy—that is the crude, oily Spanish body; inside you saw the spirit, an exquisite, yearning, knife-like thing, incised with an arabesque of a brilliant beauty and, like an arabesque, leading nowhere, consuming itself with the casuistry of its own design. The sinner goes into this Cathedral, the ecstatic cold knife penetrates him, emotion pours from him like a blood, and he is reborn a Loyola, who, passionately repentant of his adulteries, commits the greatest act of adultery there is by throwing himself into the arms of an anthropomorphic God. Poor mystics.

The naves of all cathedrals are cruel; they are the undeviating spears of the faith aimed eastward with a merciless stroke, an eye for an eye, a tooth for a tooth; the healing is in the transept, that broad human shield of the heart which deflects the merciless theological purpose, with the warm felicities of life.

As I turned to cross before the altar, a small door opened in the aisle and a priest alighted on the floor, and seeing me called out, 'Se van a cerrar.' Closing. I had been in the Cathedral two minutes.

I mounted out of the darkness into the animal glare of day. Children were kicking a football against the Cathedral door. Under the Holy Family and the saints and the prophets, the leather thudded. The corner of the far transept, I discovered, was the parish dunghill. Outside his shop an idle, floury baker sat hotly reading his paper. Down the street wobbled a man learning to ride a bicycle, reeling on with two friends supporting his nervous progress. There were old women carrying water-jars and men trailing in the dust of donkeys: the hot animal world, the heavy reeking exterior, hiding the jewelled knife within, the stab of Spain.

V. S. Pritchett, Marching Spain *(1928)*

Coming Back to Cambridge
(England 1971)

Casual, almost unnoticeable,
it happens every time you return.
Somewhere along the flat road in
you lose to voluptuous levels
between signposts to unnecessary dozing villages
every ghost of yourself but Cambridge.
Somewhere—by Fen Drayton or Dry Drayton,
by the finger pointing aimlessly to Over –
you slip into a skin that lives
perpetually in Cambridge.

It knows where you are.

As you drive you watch a workman
wheel a bicycle around a stile,
hump onto the saddle and
ride off past a field of cows.
A few stop chewing to stare.
And you know where you are even before
the landmarks (beautiful to the excluded)
begin to accumulate.
The stump of the Library.
The lupin spire of the Catholic Church.
Four spikey blossoms on King's.
The Round Church, a mushroom in this
forest of Gothic and traffic and
roses too perfect to look alive.

The river is the same—conceited,
Historic, full of the young.
The streets are the same. And around them
the same figures, the same cast with a
change of actors, move as if concentric

to a radiance without location.
The pupils of their eyes glide sideways,
apprehensive of martyrdom to which
they might not be central.
They can never be sure.
Great elations could be happening without them.

And just as the hurrying, preoccupied dons
tread the elevations of their detachment and yet
preserve an air of needing to be protected,
so, also, these wives choosing vegetables in the market,
these schoolchildren in squadrons,
these continental girl-friends and black men,
these beards, these bicycles, these
skinny boys fishing, these lovers of the pubs,
these lovers of the choirboys, these intense shrill
ladies and gaunt, fanatical, burnt-out women
are all more than this. Arrogant.
Within the compass of wistfulness.

Nothing that really matters really exists.

But the statues are alive.
You can walk in and out of the picture.
Though the mild façades harden before and
behind you like stereographs, within them
there is much to be taken for granted.
Meals and quarrels, passions and inequalities.
A city like any other, were it not for the
order at the centre and the high
invisible bridge it is built upon,
with its immense views of an intelligible human landscape
into which you never look without longing to enter;
into which you never fall without the curious struggle back.

Anne Stevenson

Commission

They were given—
'cover-ups' and 'smocks', *Top of the Pops*
if they were good, a wireless they jived to
where they could not be seen, sledges

and wedges and cross-cuts to fell trees;
nothing to eat in case they were sick,
stitches in cold blood, rosaries for pain relief;
litanies to say so that they could not talk;

a chance, from an upstairs window, to catch
a glimpse of the child they'd borne
being borne away in the back of a car,
a snapshot to keep in a prayer book with saints;

coffins for stillbirths if they were well heeled;
and shoeboxes if not, or the bare clay;
night duty when they'd no child of their own
to mind; house names to answer to

and, when they outgrew old clothes,
safety pins. They were shown,
while the council considered the issue
of heating sleeping quarters, how to scrub

parquet and tile and stone and oak to bring
labour on, and by the time it came
you could have eaten your dinner off them;
the place to sign their real names

at the bottoms of pages black with words
and sentences. They were told,

if they whispered in the night, to stand out;
to call their sanitary towels 'rabbits';

to face the blank wall when breastfeeding;
to express and use a spoon to weaken the bond;
that absolution did not stretch to them;
that, in the grand scheme of things, they were good

only for 'lying under men'; to fill, with fictional
activities, the letters they wrote that were
bundled and sent to England, then sent home,
so that the fiction of England might be maintained;

to write of digs and hops, pictures and cafés
and excursions to Brighton and Bognor Regis.
One ate moss off a drystone wall.
One had no way of knowing what

was happening when her waters broke.
One slept with her newborn for two nights
in a field her father ploughed, on account
of her people not letting her inside,

and managed to keep frost off the child.
Even among beasts she could not lie down.
One was hugging her teddy and sucking
her thumb the night she delivered her son.

Tom French

*This poem was inspired by the six volumes of the final report of the
Mother and Baby Homes Commission published in Ireland in 2020.*

Country Sounds

We really lived in the country,
In the long school Summer holidays we shouldered
Our way through a thin wooden fence straight to a field
Where the hay was high and sweet-smelling, the sun crisped it and
There were poppies and shepherd's purse and cow-parsley
And the smell of grass and the buzz and murmur of insects.
Our home was big and near enough to the city,
A beautiful university but we,
My sister and I, basked and flourished in green.
Deft with her hands always she would build
Small hay igloos. We'd sit in the dark smell
And plan an easy war with bows and arrows.
No one actually suffering of course.
For we were in a mood shaped by the huge sun
Bowling overhead.
And we were in a trance of murmurous Summer sounds,
Its music sighing and blowing,
And we learnt much all the time
Whole histories of how things thrive and spread
And we packed our imaginations with country lore
Dreams of milking and taking in the harvest.

Today this cannot be.
That field and every approach to it is built on
With houses of different designs, all showing cars.
And so our country life is a memory,
A mood and a music too.
Our counterparts today don't own a field,
Can't share our languid pleasure.
I wish I could
Offer our pleasant field to them and let
Them learn the wisdom of every Summer sound.

Elizabeth Jennings

Dappled Things
for Louis & Felix

Why are so many born patterned—
the humbug tapir, the velvet boar,
the puma kittenish in tabby stripes
before they drop their finery
and are done up into a more sombre coat?—
as my nephews were born, both
with orchid skin, pink and cream on mauve ink-mackle
like mackerel sky at evening—settling
as the blood learned more, as they became solid—
so a knot of juvenile slow-worms
in their golden nest will writhe the go-
faster stripe from their dun flanks,
shuck it—and the pup blackbird's mottle
eventually drops and makes way for the dark
plumage—its graduation robe or city suit—
more serious, it's true—and more befitting of its age—
but with a brilliant blue and jade
still carried under the wing or eyelid—

Martha Sprackland

Death

Death, thou wast once an uncouth hideous thing,
Nothing but bones,
The sad effect of sadder groans:
Thy mouth was open, but thou couldst not sing.

For we considered thee as at some six
Or ten years hence,
After the loss of life and sense,
Flesh being turned to dust, and bones to sticks.

We looked on this side of thee, shooting short;
Where we did find
The shells of fledge souls left behind,
Dry dust, which sheds no tears, but may extort.

But since our Saviour's death did put some blood
Into thy face,
Thou art grown fair and full of grace,
Much in request, much sought for as a good.

For we do now behold thee gay and glad,
As at Doomsday;
When souls shall wear their new array,
And all thy bones with beauty shall be clad.

Therefore we can go die as sleep, and trust
Half that we have
Unto an honest faithful grave;
Making our pillows either down, or dust.

George Herbert

Dominus Illuminatio Mea

In the hour of death, after this life's whim,
When the heart beats low, and the eyes grow dim,
And pain has exhausted every limb—
    The lover of the Lord shall trust in Him.

When the will has forgotten the lifelong aim,
And the mind can only disgrace its fame,
And a man is uncertain of his own name—
    The power of the Lord shall fill this frame.

When the last sigh is heaved, and the last tear shed,
And the coffin is waiting beside the bed,
And the widow and child forsake the dead—
    The angel of the Lord shall lift this head.

For even the purest delight may pall,
And power must fail, and the pride must fall,
And the love of the dearest friends grow small—
    But the glory of the Lord is all in all.

Richard Doddridge Blackmore

Hilda Doolittle's 'Trilogy' stands with Ezra Pound's 'Pisan Cantos', if not with T. S. Eliot's 'Four Quartets', as a tremendous poetic sequence written during the war of 1939-45. The following extract comes from the fourth canto of 'The Flowering of the Rod', the final section of 'Trilogy'.

Double Nostalgia

Blue-geese, white-geese, you may say,
yes, I know this duality, this double nostalgia;

I know the insatiable longing
in winter, for palm shadow

and sand and burnt sea-drift;
but in the summer, as I watch

the wave till its edge of foam
touches the hot sand and instantly

vanishes like snow on the equator,
I would cry out, stay, stay;

then I remember delicate enduring frost
and its mid-winter dawn-pattern;

in the hot noon-sun, I think of the grey
opalescent winter-dawn, as the wave

burns on the shingle, I think,
you are less beautiful than frost;

but it is also true that I pray,
O, give me burning blue

and brittle burnt sea-weed
above the tide-line

as I stand, still unsatisfied,
under the long shadow-on-snow of the pine.

H. D. (Hilda Doolittle)

This poem of 1867 has been anthologized so often that I hesitate to include it; but it is picture-perfect, and some of its images are unforgettable.

Dover Beach

The sea is calm tonight.
The tide is full, the moon lies fair
Upon the straits; on the French coast the light
Gleams and is gone; the cliffs of England stand,
Glimmering and vast, out in the tranquil bay.
Come to the window, sweet is the night-air!
Only, from the long line of spray
Where the sea meets the moon-blanch'd land,
Listen! you hear the grating roar
Of pebbles which the waves draw back, and fling,
At their return, up the high strand,
Begin, and cease, and then again begin,
With tremulous cadence slow, and bring
The eternal note of sadness in.

Sophocles long ago
Heard it on the Ægean, and it brought
Into his mind the turbid ebb and flow
Of human misery; we
Find also in the sound a thought,
Hearing it by this distant northern sea.

The Sea of Faith
Was once, too, at the full, and round earth's shore
Lay like the folds of a bright girdle furl'd.

But now I only hear
Its melancholy, long, withdrawing roar,
Retreating, to the breath
Of the night-wind, down the vast edges drear
And naked shingles of the world.

Ah, love, let us be true
To one another! for the world, which seems
To lie before us like a land of dreams,
So various, so beautiful, so new,
Hath really neither joy, nor love, nor light,
Nor certitude, nor peace, nor help for pain;
And we are here as on a darkling plain
Swept with confused alarms of struggle and flight,
Where ignorant armies clash by night.

Matthew Arnold

Dream of 1819

She dream'd of being alone on the sea-shore,
    Chain'd to a rock; she knew not how, but stir
She could not from the spot, and the loud roar
    Grew, and each wave rose roughly, threatening her;
And o'er her upper lip they seem'd to pour,
    Until she sobb'd for breath, and soon they were
Foaming o'er her lone head, so fierce and high—
Each broke to drown her, yet she could not die.

Anon—she was released, and then she stray'd
    O'er the sharp shingles with her bleeding feet,
And stumbled almost every step she made;
    And something roll'd before her in a sheet,
Which she must still pursue howe'er afraid:
    'Twas white and indistinct, nor stopp'd to meet
Her glance nor grasp, for still she gazed, and grasp'd,
And ran, but it escaped her as she clasp'd.

The dream changed: in a cave she stood, its walls
    Were hung with marble icicles, the work
Of ages on its water-fretted halls,
    Where waves might wash, and seals might breed and lurk;
Her hair was dripping, and the very balls
    Of her black eyes seem'd turn'd to tears, and mirk
The sharp rocks look'd below each drop they caught,
Which froze to marble as it fell, she thought.

Lord Byron, Don Juan, canto IV

Dream of 1943

Recently I dreamt—I don't know what I dreamt; but in the course of my dream, I saw a painting by, I understood, Botticelli, and it was a painting of angels making merry in the sky; but it wasn't the theme that struck me, for of that I have no details in my memory; it was the background. For the artist had painted the picture as if he had stood, not upon the ground, looking upwards, but himself on a level with his angels, up in the middle air; and far below lay a landskip more desolate & enchanting than ever I have seen from tower or mountain-top, a vast, dreary, unpeopled waste, over which great floods lay spread in formless patterns, coiling aimlessly this way and that in long arms and reaches over the grey treeless waste; and between it and the clear, bright air where the angels were holding their celestial conversazione, there wheeled, like drifting flakes of snow, a cloud of wild swans, with wide wings and necks outstretched, looking ever downwards, so vivid that I thought I could hear their heavy pinions whirring—the symbol of life, midway between the dead world and eternity.

Hugh Trevor-Roper, Wartime Journals

Funeral Thoughts I

Sir Christopher Mings was a naval commander who plundered Spanish ships, raided Spanish settlements in the Caribbean, and shared his spoils with his fellow buccaneers. During a battle in the North Sea a sharp-shooter aboard the Dutch flagship fatally wounded him. Samuel Pepys attended his obsequies on 13 June 1666.

Heard the service, and staid till they buried him, and then out. And there met with Sir W. Coventry (who was there out of great generosity, and no person of quality there but he) and went with him into his coach, and being in it with him there happened this extraordinary case,—one of the most romantique that ever I heard of in my life, and could not have believed, but that I did see it; which was this:—About a dozen able, lusty, proper men come to the coach-side with tears in their eyes, and one of them that spoke for the rest begun and says to Sir W. Coventry, "We are here a dozen of us that have long known and loved, and served our dead commander, Sir Christopher Mings, and have now done the last office of laying him in the ground. We would be glad we had any other to offer after him, and in revenge of him. All we have is our lives; if you will please to get His Royal Highness to give us a fireship among us all, here is a dozen of us, out of all which choose you one to be commander, and the rest of us, whoever he is, will serve him; and, if possible, do that that shall show our memory of our dead commander, and our revenge." Sir W. Coventry was herewith much moved (as well as I, who could hardly abstain from weeping), and took their names, and so parted; telling me that he would move His Royal Highness as in a thing very extraordinary, which was done. Thereon see the next day in this book. So we parted. The truth is, Sir Christopher Mings was a very stout man, and a man of great parts, and most excellent tongue among ordinary men; and as Sir W. Coventry says, could have been the most useful man at such a pinch of time as this. He was come into great renowne here at home, and more abroad in the West Indys. He had brought his family into a way of being great; but dying at this time, his memory and name (his father being always and at this day a shoemaker, and his mother a Hoyman's daughter; of which he was used frequently to boast) will be quite forgot in a few months as if he had never been.

Samuel Pepys

Funeral Thoughts II

George Odger's death on 4 March 1877 was reported by The Times: 'born in 1820 in a village between Plymouth and Tavistock, his education was limited to the rustic school of his native place, and consisted of the simplest rudiments of elementary knowledge. He commenced an early course of study and self-culture, and made himself soon known in his native county as an advanced thinker, public reader, and reciter of dramatic, poetic, and general literature.' W. E. H. Lecky likened him to Marx and Mazzini. On Saturday, 10 March his funeral procession proceeded from Bloomsbury, via Leicester Square, Piccadilly and Knightsbridge, to Brompton cemetery in Kensington. It was espied on this route by an American who had recently moved into lodgings near Piccadilly.

Mr. George Odger, it will be remembered, was an English radical agitator, of humble origin, who had distinguished himself by a perverse desire to get into Parliament. He exercised, I believe, the useful profession of shoemaker, and he knocked in vain at the door that opens but to golden keys. But he was a useful and honourable man, and his own people gave him an honourable burial. I emerged accidentally into Piccadilly at the moment they were so engaged, and the spectacle was one I should have been sorry to miss. The crowd was enormous, but I managed to squeeze through it and to get into a hansom cab that was drawn up beside the pavement, and here I looked on as from a box at the play. Though it was a funeral that was going on I will not call it a tragedy; but it was a very serious comedy. The day happened to be magnificent—the finest of the year. The funeral had been taken in hand by the classes who are socially unrepresented in Parliament, and it had the character of a great popular "manifestation." The hearse was followed by very few carriages, but the cortége of pedestrians stretched away in the sunshine, up and down the classic gentility of Piccadilly, on a scale that was highly impressive. Here and there the line was broken by a small brass band—apparently one of those bands of itinerant Germans that play for coppers beneath lodging-house windows; but for the rest it was compactly made up of what the newspapers call the dregs of the population. It was the London rabble, the metropolitan mob, men and women, boys and girls, the decent poor and the indecent, who had scrambled into the ranks as they gathered them up on their passage, and were making a sort of solemn spree of it. Very solemn it all was—perfectly proper and undemonstrative. They shuffled along in an interminable line, and as I looked at them out of the front of my hansom I seemed to be having a sort of panoramic view of the under-side, the wrong side, of the London world. The procession was filled with figures which seemed never to have "shown out," as the English say, before; of strange, pale, mouldy paupers who blinked and stumbled in the Piccadilly sunshine. I have no space to describe them more minutely, but I found in the whole affair something memorable. My impression rose not simply from the radical, or as I may say for the sake of colour, the revolutionary, emanation of this dingy concourse, lighted up by the ironical sky; but from the same causes that I had observed a short time before, on the day the queen went to open Parliament, when in Trafalgar Square, looking straight down into Westminster and over the royal cortége, were gathered a group of banners and festoons, inscribed in big staring letters with mottoes and sentiments which a sensitive police-department might easily have found seditious.

Henry James

Funeral Thoughts III

Yesterday we went to [Thomas] Hardy's funeral. What did I think of? Of Max Beerbohm's letter, just read; or a lecture to the Newnhamites about women's writing. At intervals some emotion broke in. But I doubt the capacity of the human animal for being dignified in ceremony. One catches a Bishop's frown & twitch: sees his polished shiny nose; suspects the rapt spectacled young priest gazing at the cross he carries, of being a humbug; catches Robert Lynd's distracted haggard eye; then thinks of the mediocrity of Squire [a literary journalist]; next here is the coffin, an overgrown one; like a stage coffin, covered with a white satin cloth: bearers elderly gentlemen rather red & stiff, holding to the corners: pigeons flying outside; insufficient artificial light; procession to Poet's Corner; dramatic "In sure & certain hope of immortality" ... Over all this broods for me, some uneasy sense, of change, & mortality, & how partings are deaths.

Virginia Woolf, diary 17 January 1928

Bernard Richards, of Brasenose College, Oxford, likens Woolf's mind-wandering at Hardy's funeral to a passage in John Donne's sermon at the funeral of Sir William Cockayne in 1626. Donne deplores the weak concentration of people at prayer:

> *I throw my selfe downe in my Chamber, and I call in, and invite God, and his Angels thither, and when they are there, I neglect God and his Angels, for the noise of a Flie, for the ratling of a Coach, for the whining of a doore; I talke on, in the same posture of praying; Eyes lifted up; knees bowed downe; as though I prayed to God; and, if God, or his Angels should aske me, when I thought last of God in that prayer, I cannot tell: Sometimes I finde that I had forgot what I was about, but when I began to forget it, I cannot tell. A memory of yesterdays pleasures, a feare of to-morrows dangers, a straw under my knee, a noise in mine eare, a light in mine eye, an any thing, a nothing, a fancy, a Chimera in my braine, troubles me in my prayer. So certainly is there nothing, nothing in spirituall things, perfect in this world.*

Gardener's Tale

Dog rose, waif-and-stray
cluster of torn leaves with pinky grey
soft-tissue faces; escapee
from wildwood, vacant lot or motorway
embankment; wet petals at break of day;
dropped handkerchiefs from the Rosaceae's proto-tree

filed among fossils now; little weaver
of thorns sharp enough to crown a saviour—
who dumped you in the yard beyond our gate?
June has gone by like a hidden river
and we felt the green gloom would go on forever
and suffocate us. Humboldt, the cat,

feints at a sunpatch, snakes under the fence
to a kingdom of cans and old sofas, making sense
of empty beer bottles and rubbish bags
which skirt a siding; then, at once
querying and questing, waits to pounce
on a blind vole and tear its flesh to rags.

It is time to dig deep and clean up
litter of generations who chose to stop
in this Welsh farmhouse one sly mile from England.
South-faced to give the sun a chance to soak
into the bones of the living, for summer's sake;
long-limbed, square on the hill and built to stand

in full valley view, proud and plain;
sometime a house of peacocks, Ty Bain
is our beginning for the end of life.
Grey slate and red-baked brick hang upon

oak of Montgomery—in Wales, Maldwyn:
a decent diet, like a country loaf.

The land needs clearing, colour. Forget
catalogues and garden centres. Let
the dog rose lope within the precinct. Sow
kingcup, wild garlic, poppy, marguerite
and tread the hazel cuttings underfoot
into the ground until the grasses grow.

A new neighbour owns dray horses
bred in the Black Country whose white faces
come alive with affection for our kind.
He prays they will bring home prizes
from the Angus fête though bereft of their old uses
dragging ale to the pub, coffins to church ground.

In the long light of summer you can work
through to an hour off midnight without break
but we live under the ascending flight
path of BA One-Thirteen to New York,
ever on cue to set the body clock
to a faint bee drone from twenty thousand feet

and welcome us to a meal about seven,
laughing, or not, at those whose ground is even.
High on hills westward, gorse relieves
green with chrome yellow coinage from heaven
and any moment midge- or impulse-driven
bats, not swallows, will scatter from the eaves.

Gardening bookshelves call us to the wild
(Mirabel Osler, Miriam Rothschild)
while we have earth to wrestle with and free

from cattle pens and concrete, barbed wire rolled
and lethal; and plans for burying an old
refrigerator under an apple tree.

And share creation always, from the small
menace of gastropods: slugs and snails who crawl
and slime their egress; the proliferating bat
protected by the law; from the architectural
wonder of wasp nests to this miracle:
Rosa canina and a favourite cat.

If big themes are tragic, happiness
blooms in small corners: sunlight on a dress
moving in from shadow; flood water; a call
to capture the unfolding sensuousness
of white nymphaeas or purple iris;
absurd pleasure at the steamy pile

of straw christened by horses and settling in
to rot by the compost heap, good as a win
at the races, and, best of all, the bright
certainty that in the end sins are forgiven
or rotted down themselves, season by season,
and we have laughter while we have the light.

Grey Gowrie

Ginger?

I first read the poems of A. E. Housman fifty years ago in a book that Lord Somervell of Harrow had bequeathed to the London Library. Somervell had been a Lord of Appeal in Ordinary during the 1950s, Home Secretary in 1945, Attorney General in the 1930s, and the first scientific Prize Fellow of All Souls. One of his pencil annotations was set in the margin beside a poem in which a youth goes to the gallows. In a poised and comely handwriting he had sighed, 'Oh, for the good old days when we could hang all malefactors.' Many of the young miscreants in Housman's poems were disposed to practise, in a legal phrase that Somervell will have known, 'the detestable and abominable crime of buggery (not to be named among Christians).' Hence the nameless, abominable trait of the man on the railway platform in this poem.

Oh who is that young sinner with the handcuffs on his wrists?
And what has he been after that they groan and shake their fists?
And wherefore is he wearing such a conscience-stricken air?
Oh they're taking him to prison for the colour of his hair.

'Tis a shame to human nature, such a head of hair as his;
In the good old time 'twas hanging for the colour that it is;
Though hanging isn't bad enough and flaying would be fair
For the nameless and abominable colour of his hair.

Oh a deal of pains he's taken and a pretty price he's paid
To hide his poll or dye it of a mentionable shade;
But they've pulled the beggar's hat off for the world to see and stare,
And they're haling him to justice for the colour of his hair.

Now 'tis oakum for his fingers and the treadmill for his feet,
And the quarry-gang on Portland in the cold and in the heat,
And between his spells of labour in the time he has to spare
He can curse the God that made him for the colour of his hair.

A. E. Housman

William Edward Hartpole Lecky was a nineteenth-century Irish scholar who wrote, among other works, A History of the Rise and Influence of Rationalism in Europe *in two volumes,* A History of England in the Eighteenth Century *in eight volumes, and two volumes of lordly pessimism entitled* Democracy and Liberty. *As a scholar he was industrious, untiring, even passionate. Lord Acton called his history of England 'nutritious', but thought it 'puerile' of him to write modern history drawn only from printed books. Lecky, who was elected as a MP to represent Dublin University in the Westminster parliament, was a poet who knew his own measure.*

He Found His Work

He found his work, but far behind
Lay something that he could not find:
Deep springs of passion that can make
A life sublime for others' sake,
And lend to work the living glow
That saints and bards and heroes know.
The power lay there—unfolded power—
A bud that never bloomed a flower;
For half beliefs and jaded moods
Of worldlings, critics, cynics, prudes,
Lay round his path and dimmed and chilled.
Illusions past. High hopes were killed;
But Duty lived. He sought not far
The 'might be' in the things that are;
His ear caught no celestrial strain;
He dreamed of no millennial reign.
Brave, true, unhoping, calm, austere,
He laboured in a narrow sphere,
And found in work his spirit needs—
The last, if not the best, of creeds.

W. E. H. Lecky

Henry Hastings (1561-1650)

Mr Hastings, by his quality, being son, brother, and uncle to the Earls of Huntingdon, and his way of living, had the first place amongst us. He was peradventure an original in our age, or rather the copy of our nobility in ancient days in hunting and not warlike times; he was low, very strong, and very active, of a reddish flaxen hair, his clothes always green cloth, and never all worth when new five pounds. His house was perfectly of the old fashion, in the midst of a large park well stocked with deer, and near the house rabbits to serve his kitchen, many fish-ponds, and great store of wood and timber; a bowling-green in it, long but narrow, full of high ridges, it being never levelled since it was ploughed; they used round sand bowls, and it had a banqueting-house like a stand, a large one built in a tree. He kept all manner of sport-hounds that ran; buck, fox, hare, otter, and badger, and hawks long and short winged; he had all sorts of nets for fishing: he had a walk in the New Forest and the manor of Christ Church. This last supplied him with red deer, sea and river fish; and indeed all his neighbours' grounds and royalties were free to him, who bestowed all his time in such sports, but what he borrowed to caress his neighbours' wives and daughters, there being not a woman in all his walks of the degree of a yeoman's wife or under, and under the age of forty, but it was extremely her fault if he was not intimately acquainted with her. This made him very popular, always speaking kindly to the husband, brother, or father who was to boot very welcome to his house whenever he came. There he found beef pudding and small beer in great plenty, a house not so neatly kept as to shame him or his dirty shoes, the great hall strewed with marrow bones, full of hawks' perches, hounds, spaniels, and terriers, the upper sides of the hall hung with the fox skins of this and the last year's skinning, here and there a polecat intermixed, guns and keepers' and huntsmen's poles in abundance. The parlour was a large long room, as properly furnished; on a great hearth paved with brick lay some terriers and the choicest hounds and spaniels; seldom but two of the chairs had litters of cats in them, which were not to be disturbed, he having always three or four attending him at dinner, and a little white round stick of fourteen inches long lying by his trencher, that he might defend such meat as he had no mind to part with to them. The windows, which were very large, served for places to lay his arrows, crossbows, stonebows and other suchlike accoutrements; the corners of the room full of the best chose hunting and hawking poles; an oyster-table at the lower end, which was of constant use twice a day all the year round, for he never failed to eat oysters before dinner and supper through all seasons; the neighbouring town of Poole supplied him with them. The upper part of the room had two small tables and a desk, on one side of which was a church Bible, and on the other the Book of Martyrs; on the tables were hawks' hoods, bells, and suchlike, two or three small green hats, with their crowns thrust in so as to hold ten or a dozen eggs, which were of a pheasant kind of poultry he took much care of and fed himself; tables, dice, cards and boxes were not wanting. In the hole of the desk were store of tobacco-pipes that had been used. On one side of this end of the room was the door of a closet, wherein stood the strong beer and the wine, which never came thence but in single glasses, that being the rule of the house exactly observed, for he never exceeded in drink or permitted it. On the other side was a door into an old chapel not used for devotion; the pulpit, as the safest place, was never wanting of a cold chine of beef, pasty of venison, gammon of bacon, or great apple-pie, with thick crust extremely baked. His table cost him not much, though it was very good to eat at, his sports supplying all but beef and mutton, except Friday, when he had the best sea-fish, and was the day when his neighbours of best quality visited him. He drank a glass of wine or two at meals, very often syrup of gillyflower in his sack, and always had a tun glass without feet stood by him holding a pint of small beer, which he offered stirred with a great sprig of rosemary. He was well-natured, but soon to angry, calling his servants bastards and cuckoldy knaves, in one of which he often spoke the truth to his own knowledge, and sometimes in both, though of the same man.

Anthony Ashley-Cooper, Earl of Shaftesbury

Horizon Poems

VI

Palinurus, clawing at the cliff-side,
dragged by his heavy clothes,
numb & sick from the brine,
realises the god has not lied—
he is going to die on land:
the wreckers crunch towards him
      with their boat-hooks.

VII

Smeared with weeds & clay,
stung by sand & gravel,
Prometheus wades ashore
on to this island world,
carrying a precious thing—

brazier of rubies
      from ashes of sunrise,
tenderness in his great hands

that for our sake will be nailed to blackening rock.

Sally Purcell

Humankind

Man, so far as natural science by itself is able to teach us, is no longer the final cause of the universe, the Heaven-descended heir of all the ages. His very existence is an accident, his story a brief and transitory episode in the life of one of the meanest of the planets. Of the combination of causes which first converted a dead organic compound into the living progenitors of humanity, science, indeed, as yet knows nothing. It is enough that from such beginnings famine, disease, and mutual slaughter, fit nurses of the future lords of creation, have gradually evolved, after infinite travail, a race with conscience enough to feel that it is vile, and intelligence enough to know that it is insignificant. We survey the past, and see that its history is of blood and tears, of helpless blundering, of wild revolt, of stupid acquiescence, of empty aspirations. We sound the future, and learn that after a period, long compared with the individual life, but short indeed compared with the divisions of time open to our investigation, the energies of our system will decay, the glory of the sun will be dimmed, and the earth, tideless and inert, will no longer tolerate the race which has for a moment disturbed its solitude. Man will go down into the pit, and all his thoughts will perish. The uneasy consciousness, which in this obscure corner has for a brief space broken the contented silence of the universe, will be at rest. Matter will know itself no longer. "Imperishable monuments" and "immortal deeds", death itself, and love stronger than death, will be as though they had never been. Nor will anything that *is* be better or be worse for all that the labour, genius, devotion, and suffering of man have striven through countless generations to effect.

Arthur James Balfour, Foundations of Belief *(1895)*

Balfour was our most philosophically-minded prime minister, who governed in 1902-5. His fatalism led him into careless policies and irresponsible decisions: he was, as Lord Darling wrote in a sonnet to mark his eightieth birthday,

> *Doubtful, at times, if mending be worth while*
> *Where nought persists but ordered, slow decay,*
> *Careless of hate, not wholly liking love.*

Hymn to the Sun

'Voy wawm' said the dustman
one bright August morning—
But that was in Long Benton,
under the trees.

He was Northumbrian, he'd never known
horizons shimmering in the sun,
men with swart noontide faces sleeping, thick with flies,
by roadside cherry trees.

He was Northumbrian, how should he know
mirage among blue hills,
thin streams that tinkle silence in the still
pulsating drone of summer—

How should he know
how should he know
how cool the darkness in the white-washed inns
after the white road dancing, and the stones,
and quick dry lizards, round Millevaches?

'*Fait chaud*', as each old woman said,
going over the hill, in Périgord,
prim in tight bonnets, worn black dresses, and content
with the lilt of sunlight in their bones.

Michael Roberts

Idleness

I saw old Idleness, fat, with great cheeks
Puffed to the huge circumference of a sigh,
But past all tinge of apples long ago.
His boyish fingers twiddled up and down
The filthy remnant of a cup of physic
That thicked in odour all the while he stayed.
His eyes were sad as fishes that swim up
And stare upon an element not theirs
Through a thin skin of shrewish water, then
Turn on a languid fin, and dip down, down,
Into unplumbed, vast, oozy deeps of dream.
His stomach was his master, and proclaimed it;
And never were such meagre puppets made
The slaves of such a tyrant, as his thoughts
Of that obese epitome of ills.
Trussed up he sat, the mockery of himself;
And when upon the wan green of his eye
I marked the gathering lustre of a tear,
Thought I myself must weep, until I caught
A grey, smug smile of satisfaction smirch
His pallid features at his misery.
And laugh did I, to see the little snares
He had set for pests to vex him: his great feet
Prisoned in greater boots; so narrow a stool
To seat such elephantine parts as his;
Ay, and the book he read, a Hebrew Bible;
And, to incite a gross and backward wit,
An old, crabbed, wormed, Greek dictionary; and
A foxy Ovid bound in dappled calf.

Walter de la Mare

I have been ...

I have been an actor, a money-lender, a physician, a professor of animal magnetism (that was lucrative till it went out of fashion; perhaps it will come in again); I have been a lawyer, a house-agent, a dealer in curiosities and china; I have kept a hotel, I have set up a weekly newspaper.

William Gawtrey in Bulwer-Lytton, Night and Morning *(1841)*

[Spartacus Bursch, Soho conspirator] Red Republican manufacturer of lucifer-matches, *affilié* of several secret societies, chemical lecturer, contractor for paving roads, usher in a boarding-school; then of Oran, Algeria, private soldier in the Foreign Legion; then of Burgos, Santander, St. Sebastian, and Passajes, warrior in the Spanish service, Carlist or Christino by turns; then of the United States of America, barman at a liquor store, professor of languages, and marker at a New Orleans billiard-room; subsequently and ultimately of London, promoter of a patent for extracting vinegar from white lead, keeper of a cigar-shop, professor of fencing, calisthenics, and German literature; and latterly out of any trade.

George Augustus Sala, Gaslight and Daylight *(1859)*

I have been a vagabond and a blackguard in my time, I've been a street-tumbler, a tramp, a gypsy's boy! I've sung for half-pence with dancing dogs on the high road! I've worn a footboy's livery, and waited at table! I've been a common sailors' cook, and a starving fisherman's jack-of-all-trades!

Ozias Midwinter in Wilkie Collins, Armadale *(1866)*

My present self is the outcome of all my extinct selves. I was a boatman on the Nile, a pimp in Rome at the time of the Punic wars, then a Greek orator in Suburra, where I was devoured by bed-bugs. I died during the Crusades from eating too many grapes on a beach in Syria. I have been a pirate, and a monk, a juggler and a coachman. Perhaps the Emperor of China as well?

Gustave Flaubert, letter to Georges Sands, 1866

Sea apprentice; sundowner; sailor; stock-rider; butcher; globe-trotter (record round the world, in 64½ days); schoolmaster; journalist; story-writer; treasured a pipe smoked at 19,300 feet above sea-level; found the source of the Amazon river-system; flew in a balloon from London to the field of Agincourt; last Englishman who fell there.

Who's Who entry of George Griffith, 1906

In answer to your application about my parentage, my mother was a bus-horse, my father a cab-driver, my sister a rough-rider over the Arctic regions. My brothers were all gallant sailors on a steamroller.

George Joseph Smith, the Brides-in-the-bath murderer, letter to his father-in-law, 1911

A medical student, an oarsman, a tenor, an amateur actor, a shouting politician, a small landlord, a small investor, a drinker, a good fellow, a storyteller, somebody's secretary, something in a distillery, a tax gatherer, a bankrupt, and at present a praiser of his own past.

James Joyce, Portrait of the Artist as a Young Man *(1916)*

I'm ten people! I was a teacher, student, farmer, Tsarist, murderer, and traitor. I've known peace and plenty, poverty, war, typhoid, starvation, night and day, frost and sweltering heat, danger and life.

Nikolai Brandeis in Joseph Roth, Rechts und Links *(1929)*

Since the war—when he held a commission in the Foot Guards—
he had been successively, but not successfully, a land agent (the
property was soon sold), a dealer in motor-cars (the business went
speedily bankrupt), a stockbroker on half commission, the manager
of a tourist agency, an advertisement tout, and a highly incompetent
society journalist.

Frederick Barbon in John Buchan, Castle Gay *(1930)*

Basil [Seal] had been a leader writer on the Daily Beast, he had
served in the personal entourage of Lord Monomark, he had sold
champagne on commission, composed dialogue for the cinema, and
given what was intended to be a series of talks for the BBC. Sinking
lower in the social scale he had been press agent for a female con-
tortionist, and had once conducted a party of tourists to the Italian
lakes.

Evelyn Waugh, Put Out More Flags *(1942)*

Implacable November Weather

London. As much mud in the streets as if the waters had but newly retired from the face of the earth, and it would not be wonderful to meet a megalosaurus, forty feet long or so, waddling like an elephantine lizard up Holborn Hill. Smoke lowering down from chimney-pots, making a soft black drizzle, with flakes of soot in it as big as full-grown snow-flakes gone into mourning, one might imagine, for the death of the sun. Dogs, undistinguishable in mire. Horses, scarcely better; splashed to their very blinkers. Foot passengers, jostling one another's umbrellas in a general infection of ill-temper, and losing their foot-hold at street-corners, where tens of thousands of other foot passengers have been slipping and sliding since the day broke (if the day ever broke), adding new deposits to the crust upon crust of mud, sticking at those points tenaciously to the pavement, and accumulating at compound interest.

Fog everywhere. Fog up the river, where it flows among green aits and meadows; fog down the river, where it rolls defiled among the tiers of shipping and the waterside pollutions of a great (and dirty) city. Fog on the Essex marshes, fog on the Kentish heights. Fog creeping into the cabooses of collier-brigs; fog lying out on the yards, and hovering in the rigging of great ships; fog drooping on the gunwales of barges and small boats. Fog in the eyes and throats of ancient Greenwich pensioners, wheezing by the firesides of their wards; fog in the stem and bowl of the afternoon pipe of the wrathful skipper, down in his close cabin; fog cruelly pinching the toes and fingers of his shivering little 'prentice boy on deck. Chance people on the bridges peeping over the parapets into a nether sky of fog, with fog all round them, as if they were up in a balloon, and hanging in the misty clouds. Gas looming through the fog in divers places in the streets, much as the sun may, from the spongey fields, be seen to loom by husbandman and ploughboy. Most of the shops lighted two hours before their time, as the gas seems to know, for it has a haggard and unwilling look.

The raw afternoon is rawest, and the dense fog is densest, and the muddy streets are muddiest near that leaden-headed old obstruction, appropriate ornament for the threshold of a leaden-headed old corporation, Temple Bar. And hard by Temple Bar, in Lincoln's Inn Hall, at the very heart of the fog, sits the Lord High Chancellor in his High Court of Chancery.

Charles Dickens, Bleak House *(1853)*

Inscription on a college monument

The walls of the antechapel and sanctuary of the chapel of All Souls College, Oxford bear many memorials with carved inscriptions. Often they testify to the characteristics most admired in college men: 'Brisk, acute, pious' (Montagu Burrows); 'Straightforward, pleasant, distinguished' (Sir Edward Leigh); 'circumspect, kindly and charming' (Francis Compton); 'Energetic, acute, agreeable, loving this House if ever any man did' (Sir Robert Mowbray); 'wise, energetic, affable, constant' (William Geldart); 'elegant, affable, wise, eloquent' (Sir Henry Richards); 'subtle, charming, merry, untiring in exercise of mind and body' (Francis Ysidro Edgeworth). My favourite is this:

A.M.D.G.

ET IN PIAM MEMORIAM

ARTURI HENRICI JOHNSON

EX GENEROSA STIRPE APUD HADRIANI MURUM

ORIUNDUS HUIUS COLLEGII BIS COOPTATUS

SOCIUS ET PER ANNOS FERE LV CAPELLANUS

OBIIT OXONIAE ANNIS LXXXII PAENE

CONFECTIS QUEM INTRA TRES MENSES EIUSDEM

AETATIS CONIUNX DILECTISSIMA SECUTA EST

A.S. MCMXXVII

EQUES AUCEPS PISCATOR HORTORUM CULTOR

FLORUM PISCIUM AVIUM FERARUM OMNIA

GENERA OMNEM NATURAM PERNOVIT

IN HAC UNIVERSITATE STUDIA HISTORICA

EGREGIE FOVIT ERRORUM INDAGATOR ACER

ERRANTIUM PRAECEPTOR EXORABILIS PRO RE

PRO TEMPORE HILARIS GRAVIS ARDENS

PLACABILIS ERGA COLLEGIUM ERGA AMICOS

VIR PRISCAE FIDEI PRISCAE PIETATIS

To the Greater Glory of God and in pious memory of Arthur Henry

Johnson, descended from a noble stock from near Hadrian's Wall; twice elected Fellow of this College and for almost fifty-five years, Chaplain, he died in Oxford aged nearly eighty-two—his beloved wife following him within three months at the same age—in the year of our Salvation one thousand nine hundred and twenty-seven. Rider, fowler, fisherman, gardener, he thoroughly knew all species of flower, fish, bird and beast and all their natures. Within this University he outstandingly fostered the study of history; a keen hunter of errors, but an easily appeased teacher of those who made them; merry, grave, ardent as time and matter required; a moderating influence on College and friends, a man of old-fashioned faith and old-fashioned piety.

In Such Slow Sweetness

In such slow sweetness of spirit, in such kind condescensions
Of hours and fulsome boughs, the day declines
Pastelling pale and opal skies, sharpening looks and voices.
Here's the bold bravado of almost July, here is June giving way
To everything late, hollyhocks and delphiniums,
Sweet peas and all the residents of rockeries,
Here is Summer making mankind surrender,
Wherever he can in peace,
To the pleasure of rising sap, to the laying down
Of easy flesh in the afternoon while a few
Birds bicker peacefully. We have sat still at a window
Facing West and watched the sun slip behind
Pale pink and blue and hints here and there of green.
Psalms sing in our restful minds, and near at hand
A piano allows itself to be played and its sounds
Connect our mood with what seems a kind of perfection
And echoes us back to the power of the flood-lit day.

Elizabeth Jennings

Jidda

We had the accustomed calm run to Jidda, in the delightful Red Sea climate, never too hot while the ship was moving. By day we lay in shadow; and for great part of the glorious nights we would tramp up and down the wet decks under the stars in the steaming breath of the southern wind. But when at last we anchored in the outer harbour, off the white town hung between the blazing sky and its reflection in the mirage which swept and rolled over the wide lagoon, then the heat of Arabia came out like a drawn sword and struck us speechless. It was midday; and the noon sun in the East, like moonlight, put to sleep the colours. There were only lights and shadows, the white houses and black gaps of streets: in front, the pallid lustre of the haze shimmering upon the inner harbour: behind, the dazzle of league after league of featureless sand, running up to an edge of low hills, faintly suggested in the far away mist of heat.

Just north of Jidda was a second group of black-white buildings, moving up and down like pistons in the mirage, as the ship rolled at anchor and the intermittent wind shifted the heat waves in the air. It looked and felt horrible. We began to regret that the inaccessibility which made the Hejaz militarily a safe theatre of revolt involved bad climate and un-wholesomeness.

However, Colonel Wilson, British representative with the new Arab state, had sent his launch to meet us; and we had to go ashore to learn the reality of the men levitating in that mirage .... We walked past the white masonry of the still-building water gate, and through the oppressive alley of the food market on our way to the Consulate. In the air, from the men to the dates and back to the meat, squadrons of flies like particles of dust danced up and down the sun-shafts which stabbed into the darkest corners of the booths through torn places in the wood and sackcloth awnings overhead. The atmosphere was like a bath. The scarlet leathers of the armchair on the *Lama's* deck had dyed Storrs' white tunic and trousers as bright as themselves in their damp contact of the last four days, and now the sweat running in his clothes begin to shine like varnish through the strain. I was so fascinated watching him that I never noticed the deepened brown of my khaki drill wherever it touched my body. He was wondering if the walk to the Consulate was long enough to wet me a decent, solid, harmonious colour; and I was wondering if all he ever sat on would grow scarlet as himself.

⁂

It was indeed a remarkable town. The streets were alleys, wood roofed in the main bazaar, but elsewhere open to the sky in the little gap between the tops of the lofty white-walled houses. These were built four or five storeys high, of coral rag tied with square beams and decorated by wide bow-windows running from ground to roof in grey wooden panels. There was no glass in Jidda, but a profusion of good lattices, and some very delicate chiselling on the panels of window casings. The doors were heavy two-leaved slabs of teak-wood, deeply carved, often with wickets in them; and they had rich hinges and ring-knockers of hammered iron. There was much moulded or cut plastering, and on the older houses fine stone heads and jambs to the windows looking on the inner courts.

The style of architecture was like crazy Elizabethan half-timber work, in the elaborate Cheshire fashion, but gone gimcrack to an incredible degree. House-fronts were fretted, pierced and pargetted till they looked as though cut out of cardboard for a romantic stage-setting. Every storey jutted, every window leaned one way or other; often the very walls sloped. It was like a dead city, so clean underfoot, and so quiet. Its winding, even streets were floored with damp sand solidified by time and as silent to the tread as any carpet. The lattices and wall-returns deadened all reverberation of voice. There were no carts, nor any streets wide enough for carts, no shod animals, no bustle anywhere. Everything was hushed, strained, even furtive. The doors of the houses shut softly as we passed. There were no loud dogs, no crying children: indeed, except in the bazaar, still half asleep, there were few wayfarers of any kind; and the rare people we did meet, all thin, and as it were wasted by disease, with scarred, hairless faces and screwed-up eyes, slipped past us quickly and cautiously, not looking at us. Their skimp, white robes, shaven polls with little skull-caps, red cotton shoulder-shawls, and bare feet were so same as almost to be a uniform.

The atmosphere was oppressive, deadly. There seemed no life in it. It was not burning hot, but held a moisture and sense of great age and exhaustion such as seemed to belong to no other place: not a passion of smells like Smyrna, Naples or Marseilles, but a feeling of long use, of the exhalations of many people, of continued bath-heat and sweat. One would say that for years Jidda had not been swept through by a firm breeze: that their streets kept their air from year's end to year's end, from the day they were built for so long as the houses should endure. There was nothing in the bazaars to buy.

T. E. Lawrence, Seven Pillars of Wisdom *(1926)*

Last Words

The tongues of dying men
Enforce attention like deep harmony.

Shakespeare

[To her husband the Duke of York and Albany, afterwards King James II]
Duke! Duke! Death is terrible!

Anne Hyde, 1671

Entrench! Entrench! Entrench!

Sir Henry Lawrence, at Lucknow, 1857

Lies! Lies! Lies!

Edward Trelawny, 1881

No sun. No moon. No stars.

Atkinson Grimshaw, landscape painter, 1893

Don't duck, Fred. The men don't like it, and it doesn't do any good.

Brigadier Lord Longford at Gallipoli, 1915

You are supposed to say beautiful things, and you can't.

Elizabeth, Queen of Romania, 1916

[Watching an electric storm on a Long Island beach]
Mercy, there's Miss God at it again!

Bert Savoy, drag-artist, 1923
[he was instantly struck by lightning]

Don't let it end like this! Tell them I said something.
'Pancho' Villa, Mexican revolutionary,
shot in an ambush, 1925

I knew it! I knew it! Born in a hotel room, and goddamit, died in a hotel room.
Eugene O'Neill, 1953

Kay, I can feel butterflies all over me. They're in my feet, my legs. They're rising.
Edmund Valentine White II, 1955
To which his wife replied, 'O, for Pete's sake, E.V., sit down!' He did, and died of a coronary.

I have a thousand things to do.
Lord Beveridge, 1963

[To a nun who wiped his brow as he lay in a hospital bed]
Thank you, Sister. May all your sons be bishops!
Brendan Behan, 1964

[Emerging from unconsciousness to find her sister weeping at her bedside]
O, you silly cow!
Jane Grigson, 1990

Wow!
Steve Jobs, 2011

Laventie

One would remember still
Meadows and low hill
Laventie was, as to the line and elm row
Growing through green strength wounded, as home elms grow.
Shimmer of summer there and blue autumn mists
Seen from trench-ditch winding in mazy twists.
The Australian gunners in close flowery hiding
Cunning found out at last, and smashed in the unspeakable lists.
And the guns in the smashed wood thumping and grinding.

The letters written there, and received there,
Books, cakes, cigarettes in a parish of famine,
And leaks in rainy times with general all-damning.
The crater, and carrying of gas cylinders on two sticks
(Pain past comparison and far past right agony gone)
Strained hopelessly of heart and frame at first fix.

Café-au-lait in dug-outs on Tommies' cookers,
Cursed minniewerfs, thirst in eighteen-hour summer.
The Australian miners clayed, and the being afraid
Before strafes, sultry August dusk time than Death dumber—
And the cooler hush after the strafe, and the long night wait—
The relief of first dawn, the crawling out to look at it,
Wonder divine of Dawn, man hesitating before Heaven's gate.
(Though not on Coopers where music fire took at it,
Though not as at Framilode beauty where body did shake at it)
Yet the dawn with aeroplanes crawling high at Heaven's gate
Lovely aerial beetles of wonderful scintillate
Strangest interest, and puffs of soft purest white—
Soaking light, dispersing colouring for fancy's delight.

Of Maconachie, Paxton, Tickler, and Gloucester's Stephens;
Fray Bentos, Spiller and Baker, odds and evens
Of trench food, but the everlasting clean craving
For bread, the pure thing, blessed beyond saving.
Canteen disappointments, and the keen boy braving
Bullets or such for grouse roused surprisingly through
    (Halfway) Stand-to.
And the shell nearly blunted my razor at shaving;
Tilleloy, Pauquissart, Neuve Chapelle, and mud like glue.

But Laventie, most of all, I think is to soldiers
The town itself with plane trees, and small-spa air;
And vin, rouge-blanc, chocolat, citron, grenadine:
One might buy in small delectable cafés there.
The broken church, and vegetable fields bare;
Neat French market town look so clean,
And the clarity, amiability of North French air.

Like water flowing beneath the dark plough and high Heaven,
Music's delight to please the poet pack-marching there.

Ivor Gurney

The following poem was written in 1898: its foresight is as striking as its word-painting. Its author was a privileged New Yorker, a renowned essayist much influenced by Emerson, who became an advocate of social, racial and legal reforms. While a law student at Harvard, as an act of remorse for beating-up a love-rival, he burnt off his left hand and used to display the stump as a mark of his probity.

Lines on the death of Bismarck

At midnight Death dismissed the chancellor,
But left the soul of Bismarck on his face.
Titanic, in the peace and power of bronze,
With three red roses loosely in his grasp,
Lies the Constructor. His machinery
Revolving in the wheels of destiny
Rolls onward over him. Alive, inspired,
Vast, intricate, complete, unthinkable,
Nice as a watch and strong as dynamite,
An empire and a whirlwind, on it moves,
While he that set it rolling lies so still.

Unity! Out of chaos, petty courts,
Princelings and potentates—thrift, jealousy,
Weakness, distemper, cowardice, distrust,
To build a nation: the material—
The fibres to be twisted—human strands.
One race, one tongue, one instinct. Unify
By banking prejudice, and, gaining power,
Attract by vanity, compel by fear.
Arm to the teeth: your friends will love you more,
And we have much to do for Germany.
Organized hatred, that is unity.

Prussia's a unit; Denmark's enmity
Is so much gain, and gives us all the North.
Next, humble Austria: a rapid stroke

That leaves us laurels and a policy.
Now for some chance, some—any fluke or crime
By which a war with France can be brought on:
And, God be glorified, the thing is done.
Organized hatred. That foundation reaches
The very bottom rock of Germany
And out of it the structure rises up
Bristling with arms.

'But you forget the soul,
'The universal shout, the Kaiser's name,
'Fatherland, anthems, the heroic dead,
'The discipline, the courage, the control,
'The glory and the passion and the flame—'
Are calculated by the captain's eye
Are used, subdued, like electricity
Turned on or off, are set to making roads,
Or building monuments, or writing verse,
Twitched by the inspired whim of tyranny
To make that tyranny perpetual
And kill what intellect it cannot use.

The age is just beginning, yet we see
The fruits of hatred ripen hourly
And Germany's in bondage—muzzled press,
The private mind suppressed,—while shade on shade
Is darkened o'er the intellectual sky.
And world-forgotten, outworn crimes and cries
With dungeon tongue accost the citizen
And send him trembling to his family...

Thought cannot grasp the Cause: 'tis in the abyss
With Nature's secrets. But, gigantic wreck,
Thou wast the Instrument! And thy huge limbs
Cover nine kingdoms as thou lie'st asleep.

John Jay Chapman

London Snow

When men were all asleep the snow came flying,
In large white flakes falling on the city brown,
Stealthily and perpetually settling and loosely lying,
      Hushing the latest traffic of the drowsy town;
Deadening, muffling, stifling its murmurs failing;
Lazily and incessantly floating down and down:
      Silently sifting and veiling road, roof and railing;
Hiding difference, making unevenness even,
Into angles and crevices softly drifting and sailing.
      All night it fell, and when full inches seven
It lay in the depth of its uncompacted lightness,
The clouds blew off from a high and frosty heaven;
      And all woke earlier for the unaccustomed brightness
Of the winter dawning, the strange unheavenly glare:
The eye marvelled—marvelled at the dazzling whiteness;
      The ear hearkened to the stillness of the solemn air;
No sound of wheel rumbling nor of foot falling,
And the busy morning cries came thin and spare.
      Then boys I heard, as they went to school, calling,
They gathered up the crystal manna to freeze
Their tongues with tasting, their hands with snowballing;
      Or rioted in a drift, plunging up to the knees;
Or peering up from under the white-mossed wonder,
'O look at the trees!' they cried, 'O look at the trees!'
      With lessened load a few carts creak and blunder,
Following along the white deserted way,
A country company long dispersed asunder:
      When now already the sun, in pale display
Standing by Paul's high dome, spread forth below
His sparkling beams, and awoke the stir of the day.
      For now doors open, and war is waged with the snow;

And trains of sombre men, past tale of number,
Tread long brown paths, as toward their toil they go:
          But even for them awhile no cares encumber
Their minds diverted; the daily word is unspoken,
The daily thoughts of labour and sorrow slumber
At the sight of the beauty that greets them,
          for the charm they have broken.

Robert Bridges

The following short poem is a bracing refutation of the notion that Victorians were complacent, bustling materialists. Essentially it is a prayer addressed to God describing a mood than many people know. These lines may be read at my funeral.

Lord, many times I am weary

Lord, many times I am aweary quite
Of mine own self, my sin, my vanity—
Yet be not Thou, or I am lost outright,
    Weary of me.

And hate against myself I often bear,
And enter with myself in fierce debate:
Take Thou my part against myself, nor share
    In that just hate.

Best friends might loathe us, if what things perverse,
We know of our own selves, they also knew;
Lord, Holy One! if Thou who knowest worse
    Shouldst loathe us too!

Richard Chenevix-Trench,
Archbishop of Dublin

Lough Erne, Fermanagh

All the rest of our island, three fourths of it, was a forest, chiefly of oak and ash and birch, very thick indeed. We knew it every foot; loved it in our unthinking way. Now we were Red Indians with wooden tomahawks and scalping knives and home-made bows and arrows, tracking palefaces relentlessly through the hazel scrub; now the crew of a clipper furling sails and housing the topmast high among the branches of a beech tree.

We gathered crab apples and elderberries for Mother's jelly and wine; filled a sack with hazel nuts for the festivities at Hollentide. We tracked hares over the snow, set clavens for blackbirds, snared little pike with loops of twisted hair among the bulrushes, waded through the weeds searching for waterfowls' eggs, lay for hours under the willows hoping to see an otter. If Tom, the keeper, was ferreting, we were with him. When the cranes came over to their nesting high in the ash trees in the nests, we stood laughing at sight of their legs sticking down and wondering why such silly birds chose trees as bare of scaling branches as a mast.

We cut saplings for fishing rods, forks for catapults, blackthorn and twisted walking-sticks with the woodbine still deep in the spirals; made pop-guns from elder wood by picking out the pithy core, and when the sap was up fashioned whistles from smooth ash stems after a cunning fashion. We raced, shouted, fought, played tipcat on the hill, hide-and-seek among hazels; and when, betimes, a gale went tearing through the trees our little pagan souls rejoiced. Two things we all loved much: a big wind, and the splendour of a yacht in full sail.

Shan Bullock, After Sixty Years *(1931)*

Eiléan Ní Chuilleanáin is a Fellow of Trinity College, Dublin, and emeritus professor of English literature there. She is published by the Gallery Press.

Love

The view from the train is better than a dream.
A man is gazing down his lines of beetroot,
a lone tractor waits at the level crossing,
one light glowing although it's not quite dark.
A doll has fallen into the gloom of the hedge,
her frilly skirt still white. Walls come closer,
lights on Clara station cast their orange trawl.
Beyond its margin the engines
vibrate in the car park, harmonizing the hum of love.

A newspaper spread on a dashboard
catches the last light from an office window;
a parent's overcoated shape is reading,
waiting for the noisy gang that clings
by the doors with their luggage while
the wheels are slowing and finally slide and stand.

Eiléan Ní Chuilleanáin

Amy Lowell was a poet who often failed. She strove to be remembered as an Imagist, but her work in that mode seems melodramatic, contentious, jarring, and false to me. She was too aware of her poetic mission, and too grandiloquent in her modernity. If only she had been content with traditional New England pastoral, for she had a gift for taking captive the placid moment, and a vivid sense of colour, and sincerity in her simpler moments. She addressed this poem of 1919 to the actress Ada Dwyer Russell, with whom she lived.

Madonna of the Evening Flowers

All day long I have been working:
Now I am tired.
I call: 'Where are you?'
But there is only the oak-tree rustling in the wind.
The house is very quiet,
The sun shines in on your books,
On your scissors and thimble just put down,
But you are not there.
Suddenly I am lonely:
Where are you?
I go about searching.

Then I see you,
Standing under a spire of pale blue larkspur,
With a basket of roses on your arm.
You are cool, like silver,
And you smile.
I think the Canterbury Bells are playing little tunes.

You tell me that the peonies need spraying,
That the columbines have overrun all bounds,
That the pyrus japonica should be cut back and rounded.
You tell me these things.

But I look at you, heart of silver,
White heart-flame of polished silver,
Burning beneath the blue steeples of the larkspur,
And I long to kneel instantly at your feet,
While all about us peal the loud, sweet Te Deums
    of the Canterbury bells.

Amy Lowell

March 1603

The tapestry shivers like a candle-flame
in that little wind cold as a serpent
that creeps from the grave;
the table is a dark river
reflecting silver gleams
that draw night nearer.

An old woman, dying, keeps a sword by her bed
that none dare say, The Queen is afraid,
stabs repeatedly at woven god & hunter
– or the turbulent ghosts behind them –
while their fragile figures move
through her constant looking-glass.

One night she saw her body
'lean and fearful in a light of fire';
her spirit already walks corridors
where her dead are whispering;
only they can say 'must' to princes,
and she will not ward them off much longer.

Sally Purcell

Mechanic repairing a motor-cycle

Something in the look of him makes my pulses snatch.
He crouches on the garage floor beside
The patient engine, while I stand and watch.
Black dirt and oil and loose blue clothing hide
What can be hidden. But suddenly streaming wide
The sun's rays enter through the door and catch
His neck and by their alchemy are descried
Grace and glory of youth nowhere to match!
Here is the perfect Beauty, not aware
Of its own worth, not asking homage due.
Not like those lads, whom Sculptor Myron knew,
Whose bodies proudly moved in Grecian air,
Bending to gracious play and gleaming bare.
Here's muck of toil, and Youth shines godlike through!

Sir Geoffrey Faber,
a sonnet written at Foxhall Heath, May 1916.

Alasdair Clayre was a scholar and head boy of Winchester, and a scholar of Christ Church, Oxford, who graduated with the rare distinction of a congratulatory first-class degree. After his election as a Prize Fellow of All Souls College, Oxford in 1959, he wrote a defiantly idealistic novel, The Window *(1961), at a time when most young novelists were vying to be champion cynics. He composed witty songs, recorded two musical album-records, lamented the futility of the Oxford school of linguistic philosophy, made documentary films for television, and studied workplace conditions. Through all this he became increasingly distressed, and on the publication day of his new book, threw himself in front of a tube train at Kentish Town station. This poem was a favourite of Gavin Ewart's.*

Melanie Klein's Theory

Black cypress-shadow weaves
Over the yellow globes
And seaweed-heavy leaves
Of midday grapefruit groves;
A child curls his wet tongue
Seeing such sweetness hang,
Tastes, then twists his dry-wrung
Mouth at the bitter tang.

And spits away this strange
Sweet lemon, sour orange;

But grows to reconcile
Sourer and sweeter pole,
And in a little while
Desires this new-found whole
More than the easy taste
That pleased his palate first,
And what he spat in haste
Comes to long for in thirst.

Alasdair Clayre, A Fire by the Sea *(1973)*

Midnight on the Great Western

In the third-class seat sat the journeying boy,
    And the roof-lamp's oily flame
Played down on his listless form and face,
Bewrapt past knowing to what he was going,
    Or whence he came.

In the band of his hat the journeying boy
    Had a ticket stuck; and a string
Around his neck bore the key of his box,
That twinkled gleams of the lamp's sad beams
    Like a living thing.

What past can be yours, O journeying boy,
    Towards a world unknown,
Who calmly, as if incurious quite
On all at stake, can undertake
    This plunge alone?

Knows your soul a sphere, O journeying boy,
    Our rude realms far above,
Whence with spacious vision you mark and mete
This region of sin that you find you in,
    But are not of?

Thomas Hardy

Mid-Winter Flowers

Flowers brought out of darkness, white or bruised with shade,
Jonquils and Roman hyacinths, freesias with grassy leaves,
Show the end of the year in curtained English rooms.

As white as Christmas cakes, as frost on fir and yew,
They lean through windows to the sky's unlighted plains of snow,
The winter-patient gables in the nets of trees.

But when lights are lit they dress themselves freshly.
Like faint sea-weed that crisps and dances in the risen tide,
In air of lamp-light these preen and glow, colourless.

On the oak table, earth-islanded in their bowl,
Or stilled, a fountain, in their vase, they tell our year's midnight
And turn our thoughts to east with scent and cold of dawn.

E. J. Scovell

Milk for the Cat

When the tea is brought at five o'clock,
And all the neat curtains are drawn with care,
The little black cat with bright green eyes
Is suddenly purring there.

At first she pretends, having nothing to do,
She has come in merely to blink by the grate,
But, though tea may be late or the milk may be sour,
She is never late.

And presently her agate eyes
Take a soft large milky haze,
And her independent casual glance
Becomes a stiff, hard gaze.

Then she stamps her claws or lifts her ears,
Or twists her tail and begins to stir,
Till suddenly all her lithe body becomes
One breathing trembling purr.

The children eat and wriggle and laugh;
The two old ladies stroke their silk:
But the cat is grown small and thin with desire,
Transformed to a creeping lust for milk.

The white saucer like some full moon descends
At last from the clouds of the table above;
She sighs and dreams and thrills and glows,
Transfigured with love.

She nestles over the shining rim,
Buries her chin in the creamy sea;
Her tail hangs loose; each drowsy paw
Is doubled under each bending knee.

A long dim ecstasy holds her life;
Her world is an infinite shapeless white,
Till her tongue has curled the last holy drop,
Then she sinks back into the night,

Draws and dips her body to heap
Her sleepy nerves in the great arm-chair,
Lies defeated and buried deep
Three or four hours unconscious there.

Harold Monro

Never

Never write a letter to your mistress.
Never join the Carlton Club.

Arthur Wellesley, Duke of Wellington

Never fight uneducated people except with their own weapons.

Lord Lyndhurst to Gladstone, 1843

Never retreat
Never explain.
Get it done and let them howl.

Benjamin Jowett, Master of Balliol

Never say where you have been.
Never ask for anything unless you are pretty certain to get it.

Reginald Brett, Viscount Esher

Never ask for anything.
Never refuse anything.
Never resign anything.

Arthur Johnson, chaplain of All Souls College

Never put a man entirely in the wrong if you can help it.

William Inge, dean of St Paul's cathedral

Never trust a man who hunts south of the Thames; a man who has
soup for lunch; or a man who waxes his moustache.

Sir James Richards

Never speak first to anyone you really want to know.

Villiers David

Never play cards with any man named 'Doc'.
Never eat at any place called 'Mom's'.
And never, ever, no matter what else you do in your whole life, never sleep with anyone whose troubles are worse than your own.

Nelson Algren (taught him by an old black woman)

Never sleep with anyone who has less to lose than you in being found out.

Philip, Duke of Edinburgh
(if only his second son had harked)

Nightmare of 1818

I was stared at, hooted at, grinned at, chattered at, by monkeys, by parroquets, by cockatoos. I ran into pagodas, and was fixed for centuries at the summit or in secret rooms: I was the idol; I was the priest; I was worshipped; I was sacrificed. I fled from the wrath of Brama through all the forests of Asia: Vishnu hated me: Seeva laid wait for me. I came suddenly upon Isis and Osiris: I had done a deed, they said, which the ibis and the crocodile trembled at. I was buried for a thousand years in stone coffins, with mummies and sphynxes, in narrow chambers at the heart of eternal pyramids. I was kissed, with cancerous kisses, by crocodiles; and laid, confounded with all unutterable slimy things, amongst reeds and Nilotic mud.

Thomas de Quincey,
Confessions of an Opium Eater *(1821)*

When Walter de la Mare complained of suffering nightmares during the Sudetenland crisis of 1938, his friend Eddie Meyerstein prescribed as a cure the nightly habit of looking at a lighted candle in a darkened room for a few minutes before getting into bed. Does this work?

1945

They came running over the perilous sands
    Children with their golden eyes
Crying: *Look! We have found samphire*
    Holding out their bone-ridden hands.

It might have been the spittle of wrens
    Or the silver nest of a squirrel
For I was invested with the darkness
    Of an ancient quarrel whose omens
Lay scatter'd on the silted beach.
    The children came running toward me

But I only saw the waves behind them
    Cold, salt and disastrous
Lift their black banners and break
    Endlessly, without resurrection.

Sir Herbert Read

No Continuing City

The train with its smoke and its rattle went on,
And the heavy-cheeked porter wheeled off his mixed load;
She shivered, and stood as if loth to be gone,
Staring this way and that—on the watery road,
And the inn with its arbour all naked and bleak,
And the weir churning foam, and the meaningless oast;
Till her husband turned back, and he stroked her pale cheek.
"O dear," murmured she, "must we go? but at once
   I shall never live here
   Above half a year."

And he with eyes keen as his bright singing mind,
While the cab tumbled on through the drifts of brown mist,
Shared her trouble; but knew that his future designed
A loftier life, could they meantime exist:
Then he sparkled and jested, and kissed his young sweet,
And they turned to the village, and stopped at the green,
To enter the schoolhouse with echoing feet;
And she scanned, and she planned, though she murmured between
   "I can never stay here
   Above half a year."

And now forty years of his scholars have passed,
Dunce, sluggard, and prizeman; the master remains:
He has built a new wing; and the school cap's recast;
And he makes his old jokes about beauty and brains.
And *she* speaks of home, but it is not this place,
But where a white waterfall springs down the crags,
And she goes to the garret, and stares into space,
Yet smiles when he finds her. The village tongue wags,
   "She'll never be here
   At this time next year."

         Edmund Blunden

Ocean

Roll on, thou deep and dark blue Ocean—roll!
Ten thousand fleets sweep over thee in vain;
Man marks the earth with ruin—his control
Stops with the shore;—upon the watery plain
The wrecks are all thy deed, nor doth remain
A shadow of man's ravage, save his own,
When for a moment, like a drop of rain,
He sinks into thy depths with bubbling groan,
Without a grave, unknell'd, uncoffin'd, and unknown.

His steps are not upon thy paths,—thy fields
Are not a spoil for him,—thou dost arise
And shake him from thee; the vile strength he wields
For earth's destruction thou dost all despise,
Spurning him from thy bosom to the skies,
And send'st him, shivering in thy playful spray,
And howling, to his gods, where haply lies
His petty hope in some near port or bay,
And dashest him again to earth:—there let him lay.

The armaments which thunder—strike the walls
Of rock-built cities, bidding nations quake,
And monarchs tremble in their capitals,
The oak leviathans, whose huge ribs make
Their clay creator the vain title take
Of lord of thee, and arbiter of war;
These are thy toys, and, as the snowy flake,
They melt into thy yeast of waves, which mar
Alike the Armada's pride, or spoils of Trafalgar.

Thy shores are empires, changed in all save thee—
Assyria, Greece, Rome, Carthage, what are they?
Thy waters washed them power while they were free,
And many a tyrant since: their shores obey
The stranger, slave or savage; their decay
Has dried up realms to deserts: not so thou,
Unchangeable, save to thy wild waves' play—
Time writes no wrinkle on thine azure brow—
Such as creation's dawn beheld, thou rollest now.

Thou glorious mirror, where the Almighty's form
Glasses itself in tempests; in all time,
Calm or convulsed—in breeze, or gale, or storm,
Icing the pole, or in the torrid clime
Dark-heaving;—boundless, endless, and sublime—
The image of Eternity—the throne
Of the Invisible; even from out thy slime
The monsters of the deep are made; each zone
Obeys thee; thou goest forth, dread, fathomless, alone.

Lord Byron, 'Childe Harold's Pilgrimage', canto IV

October 1943

And the rain coming down, and the rain coming down!
How lovely it falls on the rick well headed,
On potato pits thatched, on the turf clamps home,
On the roofs of the byre where the cows are bedded!

And the sun shining down, and the sun shining down!
How bright on the turnip leaves, on the stubble—
Where turkeys tip-toe across the ridges—
In this corner of peace in a world of trouble.

Patrick Kavanagh

'Of a son'

A garish room—oil-lamped; a stove's warm blaze;
Gilt chairs drawn up to candles, and green baize:
The doctor hastened in—a moment stayed,
Watching the cards upon the table played—
Club, and sharp diamond, and heart, and spade.
And—still elated—he exclaimed, '*Parbleu*,
A thousand pardons, friends, for keeping you;
I feared I'd never see the lady through.
A boy, too! *Magnifique* the fight she made!
Ah, well, she's happy now.' Said one, '"She?"—who?'
   'A woman called Landru.'

Gentle as flutter of dove's wings, the cards
Face downwards fell again; and fever-quick,
Topped by old Time and scythe, a small brass clock
In the brief hush of tongues resumed its tick.

Walter de la Mare

*Henri-Désiré Landru (1869-1922), swindler and serial killer of women,
was guillotined.*

Old Robin

Here lies old Robin: for eighty years
He tried to quench his thirst,
And tilted every flagon down
As lightly as his first:
Wines of the Arno and the Rhône,
The Tiber and the Seine,
France, Tuscany and Portugal,
He drank, but all in vain.

If every wine were spilt at once
That flowed between his lips,
They'd drown the steeple of the church
And lift a fleet of ships.
Old Robin's throat is cool at last,
His thirsty years are gone:
Beneath the yews of Bibury
No purple rivers run.

Herbert Asquith

On an Island

You've plucked a curlew, drawn a hen,
Washed the shirts of seven men,
You've stuffed my pillow, stretched my sheet,
And filled the pan to wash your feet,
You've cooped the pullets, wound the clock,
And rinsed the young men's drinking crock;
And now we'll dance to jigs and reels,
Nailed boots chasing girl's naked heels,
Until your father'll start to snore,
And Jude, now you're married, will stretch on the floor.

John Millington Synge

On the Italian Riviera

The cemetery seemed quite deserted. Gashes of overcharged daylight pressed in through the cypresses on to the graves: a hard light bestowing no grace and exacting each detail. In the shade of the pillared vaults round the walls what already seemed the dusk of evening had begun to thicken, but the rank and file of small crosses staggered arms wide in the arraignment of sunshine. In spite of the brooding repose of the trees a hundred little shrill draughts came between them, and spurting across the graves made the decorations beloved of Cordelia creak and glitter. A wreath of black tin pansies swung from the arm of a cross with a clatter of petals, trailing colourless ribbons; a beaded garland had slipped down slantwise across the foot of a grave. Candles for the peculiar glory of the lately dead had been stuck in the unhealed earth: here and there a flame in a glass shade writhed, opaque in the sunshine. Above all this uneasy rustle of remembrance, white angels poised forward to admonish. The superlatives crowding each epitaph hissed out their '*issimi*' and '*issime*' from under the millinery of death. Everywhere, in ribbons, marbles, porcelains was a suggestion of the *salon*, and nowhere could the significance of death have been brought forward more startlingly.

'I must say,' remarked Cordelia, 'I do like Italian graves; they look so much more lived in.'

'They would certainly be more difficult than others to get clear of,' said Sydney; and quickly, in unthinking perturbation, she pushed open the cemetery gates, as though she were on a message to a friend's house, and hurried in.

Elizabeth Bowen, The Hotel *(1927)*

Owed to the Tardigrade

Some of these microscopic invertebrates shrug off temperatures of minus 272 Celsius, one degree warmer than absolute zero. Other species can endure powerful radiation and the vacuum of space. In 2007, the European Space Agency sent 3,000 animals into low Earth orbit, where the tardigrades survived for 12 days on the outside of the capsule.
    —The Washington Post, *"These animals can survive until the end of the Earth, astrophysicists say"*

O, littlest un-killable one. Expert
death-delayer, master abstracter

of imperceptible flesh. We praise
your commitment to breath.

Your well-known penchant
for flexing on microbiologists,

confounding those who seek
to test your limits using ever more

abominable methods: ejection
into the vacuum of space, casting

your smooth, half-millimetre frame
into an active volcano, desiccation

on a Sunday afternoon, when the game
is on, & so many of us are likewise made

sluggish in our gait, bound to the couch
by simpler joys. *Slow-stepper,* you were

called, by men who caught first
glimpse of your eight paws walking

through baubles of rain. *Water bear.*
Moss piglet. All more or less worthy

mantles, but I watch you slink
through the boundless clarity

of a single droplet & think
your mettle ineffable, cannot

shake my adoration
for the way you hold fast

to that which is so swiftly
torn from all else living,

what you abide in order
to stay here among the flailing

& misery-stricken, the glimpse
you grant into limitless

persistence, tenacity
under unthinkable odds,

endlessness enfleshed
& given indissoluble form.

Joshua Bennett

Oxford Canal

When you have wearied of the valiant spires of this County Town,
Of its wide white streets and glistening museums, and black
monastic walls,
Of its red motors and lumbering trains, and self-sufficient people,
I will take you walking with me to a place you have not seen —
Half town and half country—the land of the Canal.
It is dearer to me than the antique town: I love it more than the
rounded hills:
Straightest, sublimest of rivers is the long Canal.
I have observed great storms and trembled: I have wept for fear of
the dark.
But nothing makes me so afraid as the clear water of this idle canal
on a summer's noon.
Do you see the great telegraph poles down in the water, how every
wire is distinct?
If a body fell into the canal it would rest entangled in those wires for
ever, between earth and air.
For the water is as deep as the stars are high.
One day I was thinking how if a man fell from that lofty pole
He would rush through the water toward me till his image was
scattered by his splash,
When suddenly a train rushed by: the brazen dome of the engine
flashed: the long white carriages roared;
The sun veiled himself for a moment, and the signals loomed in fog;
A savage woman screamed at me from a barge: little children began
to cry;
The untidy landscape rose to life: a sawmill started;
A cart rattled down to the wharf, and workmen clanged over the
iron footbridge;
A beautiful old man nodded from the first storey window of a
square red house,
And a pretty girl came out to hang up clothes in a small delightful

garden.
O strange motion in the suburb of a county town: slow regular
movement of the dance of death!
Men and not phantoms are these that move in light.
   Forgotten they live, and forgotten die.

James Elroy Flecker

Grey Gowrie first told me to read the poetry of Derek Mahon, whose work, so he promised, I would come to love and admire. Mahon was an arch formalist whose poetry mourned the loss of ceremonial habits and orderly traditions, and railed against 'progress', consumerism, despoiled landscapes and spiritual vacuity. The richness, fluency, exactitude and springiness of his vocabulary, the heart-stopping emotions, the love of truth, the surprise ambushes of his rhymes, the decisive morals that are drawn in some of his poems, must elate anyone who cares about language. Mahon's poetry made me realize, in late middle age, that it was time for serenity to replace intensity as my best temper for living. Here is a perfect miniature of lyricism by Mahon with Kent as its location.

Penshurst Place

The bright drop quivering on a thorn
in the rich silence after rain,
lute music in the orchard aisles,
the paths ablaze with daffodils,
intrigue and venery in the air
à l'ombre des jeunes filles en fleurs,
the iron hand and the velvet glove—
come live with me and be my love.

A pearl face numinously bright
shining in silence of the night,
a muffled crash of smouldering logs,
bad dreams of courtiers and of dogs,
the Spanish ships around Kinsale,
the screech owl and the nightingale,
the falcon and the turtle dove—
come live with me and be my love.

Derek Mahon

Places

How happy some places make me, Ireland for instance, and Otmoor, and many places in Gloucestershire and Northumberland, and now Coldingham, where I stayed with John and Nim Church in that delightful house of theirs which discovers itself, like the gingerbread house in the story, quite suddenly, at the end of a long ride in a wood. There I would take the dogs out, with or without a gun, and walk out of the wood and over the moor; or I would go to the top of the wood, and from the eminence there would overlook a vast distance bounded by the Cheviots on one hand and by the Lammermuirs on the other, and in front by the sea. In that clear air, all the autumn colours stood out, the colours of golden corn standing in the fields, or stubble-fields dotted with cornshocks, or green pasture, or moor in heather-flower; and there was a pastoral loneliness, that most exquisite loneliness, that Lucretius so happily describes.

Per loca pastorum deserta atque otia dia,

that is emphasised rather than broken by the noise of rooks and pigeons and curlews. And I had the same sensation, the sensation of physical delight in places, when cub-hunting the other day with the Bicester in Tittershall Wood. I arrived late, having hitch-hiked early in the morning from Aylesbury on a milk-lorry, and saddled and bridled my mare at the Crooked Billet, and as I rode up to Tittershall, the whole wood was ringing with a rising and falling note, as of seagulls around a ship, the cry of hounds hunting hither and thither through the covert. It was a beautiful morning in September; the trees were heavy with leaves; the autumn flowers, willow-herb and scabious, were out in the woodland rides; and the berries of bryony and woody-nightshade hung in the hedgerows. There again I enjoyed that delicious sensation, which is one of the choicest pleasures, that rapture that Izaak Walton meant when he quoted,

whence I know not,
I was that instant lifted above earth
And possess'd joys not promised in my birth.

Hugh Trevor-Roper, Wartime Journals

Poor Poll

I saw it all, Polly, how when you had call'd for sop
and your good friend the cook came & fill'd up your pan
you yerk'd it out deftly by beakfuls scattering it
away far as you might upon the sunny lawn
then summon'd with loud cry the little garden birds
to take their feast. Quickly came they flustering around
Ruddock & Merle & Finch squabbling among themselves
nor gave you thanks nor heed while you sat silently
watching, and I beside you in perplexity
lost in the maze of all mystery and all knowledge
felt how deep lieth the fount of man's benevolence
if a bird can share it & take pleasure in it.
  If you, my bird, I thought, had a philosophy
it might be a sounder scheme than what our moralists
propound: because thou, Poll, livest in the darkness
which human Reason searching from outside would pierce,
but, being of so feeble a candlepower, can only
show up to view the cloud that it illuminates.
Thus reason'd I: then marvell'd how you can adapt
your wild bird-mood to endure your tame environment
the domesticities of English household life
and your small brass-wire cabin, who shdst live on wing
harrying the tropical branch-flowering wilderness:
Yet Nature gave you a gift of easy mimicry
whereby you have come to win uncanny sympathies
and morsell'd utterance of our Germanic talk
as schoolmasters in Greek will flaunt their hackney'd tags
φωναντα ὀυνετοίσω and κτῆμα ἐς ἀεί
Η γλῶσσ᾽ ὀμώμοχ᾽, η δὲ Φρήν ἀνώμτος
tho' you with a better ear copy us more perfectly
nor without connotation as when you call'd for sop
all with that stumpy wooden tongue & vicious beak

that dry whistling shrieking tearing cutting pincer
now eagerly subservient to your cautious claws
exploring all varieties of attitude
in irrepressible blind groping for escape
—a very figure & image of man's soul on earth
the almighty cosmic Will fidgetting in a trap—
in your quenchless unknown desire for the unknown life
of which some homely British sailor robb'd you, alas!
'Tis all that doth your silly thoughts so busy keep
the while you sit moping like Patience on a perch
—*Wie viele Tag' und Nächte bist du geblieben*
La possa delle gambe posta in tregue—
the impeccable spruceness of your grey-feather'd pôll
a model in hairdressing for the dandiest old Duke
enough to qualify you for the House of Lords
or the Athenaeum Club to poke among the nobs
great intellectual nobs and literary nobs
scientific nobs and Bishops *ex officio* :
nor lack you simulation of profoundest wisdom
such as men's features oft acquire in very old age
by mere cooling of passion & decay of muscle
by faint renunciation even of untold regrets;
who seeing themselves a picture of that wh: man should-be
learn almost what it were to be what they are-not.
But you can never have cherish'd a determined hope
consciously to renounce or lose it, you will live
your threescore years & ten idle and puzzle-headed
as any mumping monk in his unfurnish'd cell
in peace that, poor Polly, passeth Understanding—
merely because you lack what we men understand
by Understanding. Well! well! that's the difference
C'est la seule différence, mais c'est important.
Ah! your pale sedentary life! but would you change?
exchange it for one crowded hour of glorious life,

one blind furious tussle with a madden'd monkey
who would throttle you and throw your crude fragments away
shreds unintelligible of an unmeaning act
dans la profonde horreur de l'éternelle nuit?
Why ask? You cannot know. 'Twas by no choice of yours
that you mischanged for monkeys' man's society,
'twas that British sailor drove you from Paradise—
Εἴϑ' ὠΦελ' Ἀργοῦς μή διαπτάσϑαι σκάφς!
I'd hold embargoes on such a ghastly traffic.
    I am writing verses to you & grieve that you shd be
absolument incapable de les comprendre,
Tu, Polle, nescis ista nec potes scire:—
Alas! Iambic, scazon and alexandrine,
spondee or choriamb, all is alike to you—
my well-continued fanciful experiment
wherein so many strange verses amalgamate
on the secure bedrock of Milton's prosody:
not but that when I speak you will incline an ear
in critical attention lest by chánce I míght
póssibly say sómething that was worth repeating:
I am adding (do you think?) pages to literature
that gouty excrement of human intellect
accumulating slowly & everlastingly
depositing, like guano on the Peruvian shore,
to be perhaps exhumed in some remotest age
(piis secunda, vate me, detur fuga)
to fertilize the scanty dwarf'd intelligence
of a new race of beings the unhallow'd offspring
of them who shall have quite dismember'd & destroy'd
our temple of Christian faith & fair Hellenic art
just as that monkey would, poor Polly, have done for you.

Robert Bridges

I include this poem for the sake of the birds in it, and of the mumping monk, and the Peruvian shore. It was published in the same year as The Waste Land, 1922. I wonder if its snatches of ancient and modern European languages are a tease or a tribute to T. S. Eliot. As to the Athenaeum, there has been a sorry degradation in recent years. The apostles of equality, diversity and inclusion are extruding intellectual, literary and scientific nobs. Nowadays its drawing-room is often dominated by complacent mediocrities who have been bitten by the money bug and are talking business with self-important urgency.

Rolling Stones

A near despotism, without morals or principles, such as Pandolfo Petrucci exercised from after 1490 in Siena, then torn by faction, is hardly worth a closer consideration. Insignificant and malicious, he governed with the help of a law professor and an astrologer, and frightened the people by an occasional murder. His favourite pastime in the summer months was to roll blocks of stone from the top of Monte Amiata, without caring what or whom they hit. After succeeding, where the most prudent failed, in escaping from the devices of Cesare Borgia, he at last died forsaken and despised.

Jacob Burckhardt,
Civilization of the Renaissance in Italy *(1860)*

I felt a wrench of loss at the news that Francis Hope was among the 346
people killed when an ill-designed DC10 airliner travelling from Orly
airport in Paris crashed into the forest of Ermenonville in March 1974.
For some years I had been delighted and guided by the irony, poise and
learning in his poems and book reviews: Ian Hamilton recalled the
pieces in the Observer *and* New Statesman *as 'deft, sardonic and val-*
uably unenchantable throughout the dopey Sixties.' He and the equally
short-lived Alasdair Clayre, who is also represented in this anthology,
had been elected together as Prize Fellows of All Souls in 1959.

Schlossbesuch

Behind the frayed red velvet rope we stand
Craning our necks like birds; and at my side
A child imprisoned by his mother's hand
Shuffles his feet, pulls faces at the guide.

'The picture on the left records the marriage
Of Countess Charlotte to a Spanish prince;
Her father gave the pair a rosewood carriage
Which their descendants rode in ever since.'

The sunbeams run their fingers through the dust,
Touching the heavy curtains from their gloom;
The armchairs' mouths gape wide; and Goethe's bust
Stares coldly at the unresponsive room.

'Count Michael bought the chandelier from Rome,
Each piece wrapped separately; and up these stairs
We reach the gallery of the pleasure-dome
Where mad Aunt Sophie used to say her prayers.'

And in this room the Archduke signed his papers,
And here, with suitably thick walls between,
His lace-frilled children cut Teutonic capers,
Played with their model farm, and read Racine.

Lagging behind, I stare through dirty glass
At sunshine on the gravelled walk beyond,
At the haphazard heaps of new-cut grass,
The Triton in the ornamental pond;

Then, forehead against the pane, I suddenly feel
The longing open-armed behind the bone
To drown myself in other worlds, to steal
All lives, all times, all countries not my own.

Francis Hope

Sheep-herding

In an hour or two we came to Yosemite Creek, the stream that makes the greatest of all the Yosemite falls. It is about forty feet wide at the Mono Trail crossing, and now about four feet in average depth, flowing about three miles an hour. The distance to the verge of the Yosemite wall, where it makes its tremendous plunge, is only about two miles from here. Calm, beautiful, and nearly silent, it glides with stately gestures, a dense growth of the slender two-leaved pine along its banks, and a fringe of willow, purple spirea, sedges, daisies, lilies, and columbines. Some of the sedges and willow boughs dip into the current, and just outside of the close ranks of trees there is a sunny flat of washed gravelly sand which seems to have been deposited by some ancient flood ....

The drivers and dogs had a lively, laborious time getting the sheep across the creek, the second large stream thus far that they have been compelled to cross without a bridge; the first being the North Fork of the Merced near Bower Cave. Men and dogs, shouting and barking, drove the timid, water-fearing creatures in a close crowd against the bank, but not one of the flock would launch away. While thus jammed, the Don and the shepherd rushed through the frightened crowd to stampede those in front, but this would only cause a break backward, and away they would scamper through the stream-bank trees and scatter over the rocky pavement. Then with the aid of the dogs the runaways would again be gathered and made to face the stream, and again the compacted mass would break away, amid wild shouting and barking that might well have disturbed the stream itself and marred the music of its falls, to which visitors no doubt from all quarters of the globe were listening. "Hold them there! Now hold them there!" shouted the Don; "the front ranks will soon tire of the pressure, and be glad to take to the water, then all will jump in and cross in a hurry." But they did nothing of the kind; they only avoided the pressure by breaking back in scores and hundreds, leaving the beauty of the banks sadly trampled.

If only one could be got to cross over, all would make haste to follow; but that one could not be found. A lamb was caught, carried across, and tied to a bush on the opposite bank, where it cried piteously for its mother. But though greatly concerned, the mother only called it back. That play on maternal affection failed, and we began to fear that we should be forced to make a long roundabout drive and cross the wide-spread tributaries of the creek in succession. This would require several days, but it had its advantages, for I was eager to see the sources of so famous a stream. Don Quixote, however, determined that they must ford just here, and immediately began a sort of siege by cutting down slender pines on the bank and building a corral barely large enough to hold the flock when well pressed together. And as the stream would form one side of the corral he believed that they could easily be forced into the water.

In a few hours the enclosure was completed, and the silly animals were driven in and rammed hard against the brink of the ford. Then the Don, forcing a way through the compacted mass, pitched a few of the terrified unfortunates into the stream by main strength; but instead of crossing over, they swam about close to the bank, making desperate attempts to get back into the flock. Then a dozen or more were shoved off, and the Don, tall like a crane and a good natural wader, jumped in after them, seized a struggling wether, and dragged it to the opposite shore. But no sooner did he let it go than it jumped into the stream and swam back to its frightened companions in the corral, thus manifesting sheep-nature as unchangeable as gravitation. Pan with his pipes would have had no better luck, I fear. We were now pretty well baffled. The silly creatures would suffer any sort of death rather than cross that stream. Calling a council, the dripping Don declared that starvation was now the only likely scheme to try, and that we might as well camp here in comfort and let the besieged flock grow hungry and cool, and come to their senses, if they had any. In a few minutes after being thus let alone, an adventurer in the foremost rank plunged in and swam bravely to the farther shore. Then suddenly all rushed in pell-mell together, trampling one another under water, while we vainly tried to hold them back. The Don jumped into the thickest of the gasping, gurgling, drowning mass, and shoved them right and left as if each sheep was a piece of floating timber. The current also served to drift them apart; a long, bent column was soon formed, and in a few minutes all were over and began baaing and feeding as if nothing out of the common had happened. That none were drowned seems wonderful. I fully expected that hundreds would gain the romantic fate of being swept into Yosemite over the highest waterfall in the world.

John Muir, My First Summer in the Sierra *(1911)*

'Don't keep me. Let me go.' These were the final words of Charlotte Mew after swallowing a toxic disinfectant in 1928. Her poems showed her engrossment by the subject of death, the solace that she found in loving natural beauty, and her apprehension of loss. This poem illustrates her death-wish: 'The Trees are Down', which I quote later, shows her other emotional traits.

Smile, Death

Smile, Death, see I smile as I come to you
Straight from the road and the moor that I leave behind,
Nothing on earth to me was like this wind-blown space,
Nothing was like the road, but at the end there was a vision or a face
And the eyes were not always kind.

Smile, Death, as you fasten the blades to my feet for me,
On, on let us skate past the sleeping willows dusted with snow;
Fast, fast down the frozen stream, with the moor and the road and the vision behind,
(Show me your face, why the eyes are kind!)
And we will not speak of life or believe in it or remember it as we go.

Charlotte Mew

Some Waves

Descending Portstewart Strand
the drumming wakes some dormant cell,
the need to bear the push and pull

of time. A splash of sun makes all
the difference. Strawberries and wild thyme
reach across the dunes, vying

like common blues and small heaths
that glimmer and then are gone.
Waymarked trails weave their way

through grassy spears, pointing
to bee orchids and stoned-looking bees.
The swell in the sternum

is part and parcel of being
up in this north wind, how it serves
to whip thought and enshrine

the logic that life is transitory.
Put your ear to the wind and Mahon
sings from up in Portrush.

Such quality of light, crowded
like the sky in a Paul Henry.
The beach opens like parenthesis,

its single bracket facing a depth
of field of such gravity
it's hard not to register a little panic.

Let the wrack at the edge be.
Let the moon caress your feet
the way it did when you were small.

Kevin Graham

Sonnet XII

I did but prompt the age to quit their clogs
    By the known rules of ancient liberty,
    When straight a barbarous noise environs me
    Of owls and cuckoos, asses, apes and dogs:
As when those hinds that were transform'd to frogs
    Rail'd at Latona's twin-born progeny
    Which after held the sun and moon in fee.
    But this is got by casting pearl to hogs,
That bawl for freedom in their senseless mood,
    And still revolt when truth would set them free.
    Licence they mean when they cry liberty;
    For who loves that, must first be wise and good.
But from that mark how far they rove we see,
For all this waste of wealth and loss of blood.

John Milton

Sorrow of a condemned man

Sir Everard Digby was hung, drawn and quartered in 1606 for his part in Guy Fawkes' plot to place a Catholic on the English throne. These lines were written in the Tower of London shortly before he went to the gallows. His son Kenelm was not yet three.

When on my little Babes I think, as I do oft,
I cannot choose but then let fall some tears:
Me-thinks I hear the little Pratler, with words soft,
Ask, Where is Father that did promise Pears,
And other Knacks, which I did never see,
Nor Father neither, since he promis'd me.

Spraying the Potatoes

The barrels of blue potato-spray
Stood on a headland of July
Beside an orchard wall where roses
Were young girls hanging from the sky.

The flocks of green potato-stalks
Were blossom spread for sudden flight,
The Kerr's Pinks in frivelled blue,
The Arran Banners wearing white.

And over that potato-field
A lazy veil of woven sun,
Dandelions growing on headlands, showing
Their unloved hearts to everyone.

And I was there with a knapsack sprayer
On the barrel's edge poised. A wasp was floating
Dead on a sunken briar leaf
Over a copper-poisoned ocean.

The axle-roll of a rut-locked cart
Broke the burnt stick of noon in two.
An old man came through a corn-field
Remembering his youth and some Ruth he knew.

He turned my way. 'God further the work'.
He echoed an ancient farming prayer.
I thanked him. He eyed the potato-drills.
He said: 'You are bound to have good ones there'.

We talked and our talk was a theme of kings,
A theme for strings. He hunkered down
In the shade of the orchard wall. O roses,
The old man dies in the young girl's frown.

And poet lost to potato-fields,
Remembering the lime and copper smell
Of the spraying barrels he is not lost
Or till blossomed stalks cannot weave a spell.

Patrick Kavanagh

Sara Berkeley was born in Dublin in 1967, and spent her childhood in Ireland. She concluded her education at Trinity College, Dublin and Southbank University at Elephant & Castle. After thirty years in Marin county in the San Francisco bay, where she worked as a technical editor for a computer software company, she moved to the opposite side of the continent. As described in her poems 'Covid Migration', 'Clinton Hollow' and 'Dutchess 18', she lives in a converted barn in a hamlet in upstate New York's Hudson valley. She describes her paid work as a hospice nurse and her grief at the human-made damage to the planet's climate in 'Hospice Nurse' and 'Okjökull'. Her poems are generous gifts to her readers.

Ten to Six

Ten to six,
light is leaving the full belly of the creek
but before it leaves
it picks out the loose snow
thrown by the hand of the wind,
fires it in rose gold, amber gold and, finally,
bronze. Then it is gone.
Without it the trees suffer and grow old,
the snow between the trees
turns blue with cold, wolves prowl,
the shapes of bears
cut themselves out of stone.

At dawn
it comes around again. Payne's grey
runs cool in the creek's veins
and across its liquid skin.
Geese at the water's edge feel it
shiver over their feathers,
and I watch it tune up the colours

of our waterlogged world.

I who was raised by ocean
and know in my bones the steely sea,
white caps and white dots of cottages,
thatches of vivid grass, dance of sun
and cloud, sun and cloud—
I am learning a new vernacular,
a land of ponds and streams,
pen and ink trees against the white air,
snatches of snow on a stone stair,
stone walls, red barns, and winter
moving from heavy
to middle weight
to feather light.

Sara Berkeley

Testament of a Man Forbid

They bade me then proclaim
How seemed the World now in my penitence.
But when I rose to speak, their palaces,
Their brothels, slums, cathedrals, theatres,
Asylums, factories, exchanges, banks,
The patched-up world of heirlooms, hand-me-downs
That worm and moth dispute, of make-believe,
Of shoddy, pinchbeck, sweepings of the street,
Of war disguised, of unconcealed chicane,
Of shrivelled drudge and swollen parvenu,
Turned at my glance into that murky vale
Where patient hodmen on their rounded backs
Sustained the thought of thirty centuries,
Where multitudes of slaves renounced their rest
To balance libraries upon their polls;
Or to that giant oaf (for vision shifts
The world about like winds that shape the clouds)
Whose spiritual tail, most awkward now
That breeches hide the rump, is cherished still
With ursine piety; or to that bower
Of Heaven's Delight whose barbed and cancerous roots
Are struck in earthly soil enriched with blood
Of men and women.

John Davidson

The burning Babe

As I in hoarie Winters night
      Stoode shivering in the snow,
Surpris'd I was with sodaine heate,
      Which made my hart to glow;

And lifting up a fearefull eye,
      To viewe what fire was neare,
A pretty Babe all burning bright
      Did in the ayre appeare;

Who scorched with excessive heate,
      Such floods of teares did shed,
As though his floods should quench his flames,
      Which with his teares were fed:

Alas (quoth he) but newly borne,
      In fierie heates I frie,
Yet none approach to warme their harts,
      Or feele my fire, but I;

My faultlesse breast the furnace is,
      The fuell wounding thornes:
Love is the fire, and sighs the smoake,
      The ashes, shame and scornes;

The jewell Justice layeth on,
      And Mercie blowes the coales,
The metall in this furnace wrought,
      Are mens defiled soules:

For which, as now on fire I am
>To worke them to their good,
So will I melt into a bath,
>To wash them in my blood.

With this he vanisht out of sight,
>And swiftly shrunk away,
And straight I called unto minde,
>That it was Christmasse day.

Robert Southwell,
canonised as a Saint, 1970

'I didn't see him often,' Logan Pearsall Smith wrote after Laurence Binyon's death in 1943, 'but the thought that he was there, raking up leaves in his garden or translating Dante in the big library of his little farmhouse in Berkshire, made England, made the world, seem a better place to live in. He was the last of a noble line of lovers of perfection, Milton, Wordsworth, Pater ... & Robert Bridges.' It is telling that Pearsall Smith pictured Binyon raking leaves at Westridge Green: for one of Binyon's last poems, written in response to the Blitz on south-eastern England, is entitled 'The Burning of the Leaves'. I savour the lyricism with which, in other poems, Binyon describes scenery as varied as those of Angkor, Deptford and Montenegro, even if some of his fine thinking makes me restive. 'The Burning of the Leaves', though, is a transcendent work. Because of the aerial bombardment, so he wrote, 'Truth, justice, love, beauty, the human smile' were being 'all flung to the flames!' Here is the first of the five sections of this long poem, which Binyon wrote shortly before his death. It was published posthumously.

The Burning of the Leaves

Now is the time for the burning of the leaves.
They go to the fire; the nostril pricks with smoke
Wandering slowly into a weeping mist.
Brittle and blotched, ragged and rotten sheaves!
A flame seizes the smouldering ruin and bites
On stubborn stalks that crackle as they resist.

The last hollyhock's fallen tower is dust;
All the spices of June are a bitter reek,
All the extravagant riches spent and mean.
All burns! The reddest rose is a ghost;
Sparks whirl up, to expire in the mist: the wild
Fingers of fire are making corruption clean.

Now is the time for stripping the spirit bare,
Time for the burning of days ended and done,
Idle solace of things that have gone before:
Rootless hope and fruitless desire are there;
Let them go to the fire, with never a look behind.
The world that was ours is a world that is ours no more.

They will come again, the leaf and the flower, to arise
From squalor of rottenness into the old splendour,
And magical scents to a wondering memory bring;
The same glory, to shine upon different eyes.
Earth cares for her own ruins, naught for ours.
Nothing is certain, only the certain spring.

Laurence Binyon

Jonathan Price agreed to the publication of his single volume of poetry,
Everything Must Go, *only when he knew that he was mortally ill. This*
poem was first published in the New Statesman in 1967.

The Camp

From up here note the logic of the plan,
The huts aligned like entries in a ledger,
The barriers ruled from watch-towers at the corners:
A bird's-eye view of the neat work of man.

Come down to earth now; stand inside the fence
(Voyeur or pilgrim in a place abandoned
By human kind). Survey from a new angle
The towers' commanding height, the barbed-wire tense

Over a quarter-century from when
The fences first went up (and prudent neighbours
Saw what the skylark saw; chose to see nothing).
Follow the road between the huts again.

Recall the papers that almost beyond belief
Branded for life good neighbours without number,
Peopled these paths where the thin leaves now whisper
Names, ages, annals of guilt or grief.

Track with the cameras across the square
To concrete buildings which you never entered
And from which none returned. All human nature
Shares the account of what went on in there.

Flinch, then, and fly (as only tourists can)
To join the hand-washers, and the survivors;
At a safe distance with the babbling skylark
Note the appalling logic of the plan.

Jonathan Price

The Convergence of the Twain
(Lines on the loss of the 'Titanic')

I

In a solitude of the sea
Deep from human vanity,
And the Pride of Life that planned her, stilly couches she.

II

Steel chambers, late the pyres
Of her salamandrine fires,
Cold currents thrid, and turn to rhythmic tidal lyres.

III

Over the mirrors meant
To glass the opulent
The sea-worm crawls — grotesque, slimed, dumb, indifferent.

IV

Jewels in joy designed
To ravish the sensuous mind
Lie lightless, all their sparkles bleared and black and blind.

V

Dim moon-eyed fishes near
Gaze at the gilded gear
And query: 'What does this vaingloriousness down here?' ...

VI

Well: while was fashioning
This creature of cleaving wing,
The Immanent Will that stirs and urges everything

VII

Prepared a sinister mate
For her — so gaily great —
A Shape of Ice, for the time far and dissociate.

VIII

And as the smart ship grew
In stature, grace, and hue,
In shadowy silent distance grew the Iceberg too.

IX

Alien they seemed to be:
No mortal eye could see
The intimate welding of their later history,

X

Or sign that they were bent
By paths coincident
On being anon twin halves of one august event,

XI

Till the Spinner of the Years
Said 'Now!' And each one hears,
And consummation comes, and jars two hemispheres.

Thomas Hardy

The Cranes

We thought they were gulls at first, while they were distant—
The two cranes flying out of a normal morning.
They circled twice about our house and sank,
Their long legs drooping, down over the wood.
We saw their wings flash white, frayed at the black tip,
And heard their harsh cry, like a rusty screw.
Down in the next field, shy and angular,
They darted their long necks in the grass for fish.
They would not have us close, but shambled coyly,
Ridiculous, caught on the ground. Yet our fields
Under their feet became a fen: the sky
That was blue July became watery November,
And echoing with the cries of foreign birds.

Anne Ridler

The Door

Distracting rays were shining round my door
And so I stood
And stepped across the landing floor
To see if any light-source could
Be ascertained but, once I was outside,
I checked my stride.

Out there I found a stretching corridor,
So down I walked.
I had not noticed it before.
On every lintel, names were chalked
And soon I stalled at one that was well-known:
It was my own.

The hinges creaked. I cautiously went in,
Enjoying there
A room where sunlight lapped my skin
And central was a swivel chair.
It spun about. I felt a smile extend:
'Good morning, friend.'

This figure gestured me towards an arch
Marked 'Happiness'
And I, determined, moved to march
Its way, but paused: 'I should express
Some thanks—' my friend, however, waved and said,
'You go ahead.'

Once I had ventured in I felt betrayed,
As I discerned
A maze of winding walls that made
Me dizzy, sad, until I turned
One corner and (in hope of what?) I saw
Another door.

Eager, I entered, to a gallery
Closely comprised
Of portals, each a vacancy
For liberty. I realised
I'd never loved a room. It is the door
That I adore.

Andrew Wynn Owen

The Eleven-Sided Room

The story-teller sat beside me in the window-seat, her friendly eyes in mine; and she must have felt pleased at the success of her tale. It was surely suitable and interesting, the very story for a child—no doubt she had told it to scores. I wonder who she was; she little suspected how I was to pay for that story. The fiery house, the flames shooting from the windows, must have happened to press upon some sensitive spot in a small imagination, straining or wounding it. The memory became a dread, a monstrosity, that haunted me for long—for years, as it seems to me now. It began with that session in the window-seat, in the greyish evening light, when a kind stranger took the trouble to entertain a child.

It began there, and it returned, night after night, in the room where the children slept. That indeed was an odd and disconcerting room for the calmest imagination. The Eleven-Sided Room—so it was called, and there was no doubt about its eleven distinct walls and angles; we often counted them. It might have represented the space which the builder happened to find upon his hands, when he had provided the other rooms in their order. It was full of slopes and projections, recesses, yawning cupboards like caves. An extemporized wooden staircase had been pierced to the nursery below; and there was another door that opened on to a deserted and resonant upper landing, and there were more doors that concealed strange alcoves; and between them you felt utterly exposed and powerless. You could not watch them all, you could not be on your guard in all directions at once. A candle on the mantel-piece gave just enough light to show how dark the corners were. The long hours were urgent with horror—surely half the night had gone, surely it must be near the dawn; yet still there was the sound of plates and forks and voices in the nursery below—far away, in the world of company and light, at the foot of the wooden staircase—and our nurse was still at her supper, gossiping with our grandmother's dear affectionate maid. Down there was security and peace, and tender hearts, moreover, that would have been lavished to protect and comfort a frightened child, if only—if only they could be made to understand. But alone up there among the shadows, how could you make them understand? Where could you begin with any explanation? It was hopeless; but perhaps there were feints and ruses that might bring one of them up the wooden stairs, and a few minutes of safe company might be secured in that way. Sometimes it could be managed, but not often, and not for long. Silence, solitude must be faced, and the blaze of that horrible house, with the flames leaping from its window-sockets as soon as one's eyes were shut. Hours and hours dragged on, the dawn delayed.

The soft roo-hooing of pigeons on the roof, a great splash of sun slanting through the window, life and freedom and daylight were all around one in a moment. It was another room, another world in the morning.

Percy Lubbock, Earlham *(1922)*

Is this poem, which was written in the 1940s, a retort to Arnold's 'Dover Beach'? Does the brave ship, coming home like a lamb to the fold, represent resurgent Christian faith?

The Estuary

Light, stillness and peace lie on the broad sands,
On the salt-marshes the sleep of the afternoon.
The sky's immaculate; the horizon stands
Steadfast, level and clear over the dune.

There are voices of children, musical and thin,
Not far, nor near, there in the sandy hills;
As the light begins to wane, so the tide comes in,
The shallow creek at our feet silently fills:

And silently, like sleep to the weary mind,
Silently, like the evening after the day,
The big ship bears inshore with the inshore wind,
Changes her course, and comes on up through the bay,

Rolling along the fair deep channel she knows,
Surging along, right on top of the tide.
I see the flowery wreath of foam at the bows,
The long bright wash streaming away from her side:

I see the flashing gulls that follow her in,
Screaming and tumbling, like children wildly at play,
The sea-born crescent arising, pallid and thin,
The flat safe twilight shore shelving away.

Whether remembered or dreamed, read of or told,
So it has dwelt with me, so it shall dwell with me ever:
The brave ship coming home like a lamb to the fold,
Home with the tide into the mighty river.

Ruth Pitter

The Excursion

And with their freight homeward the shepherds moved
Through the dull mist, I following—when a step,
A single step, that freed me from the skirts
Of the blind vapour, opened to my view
Glory beyond all glory ever seen
By waking sense or by the dreaming soul!
The appearance, instantaneously disclosed,
Was of a mighty city—boldly say
A wilderness of building, sinking far
And self-withdrawn into a boundless depth,
Far sinking into splendour—without end!
Fabric it seemed of diamond and of gold,
With alabaster domes, and silver spires,
And blazing terrace upon terrace, high
Uplifted; here, serene pavilions bright,
In avenues disposed; there, towers begirt
With battlements that on their restless fronts
Bore stars—illumination of all gems!
By earthly nature had the effect been wrought
Upon the dark materials of the storm
Now pacified; on them, and on the coves
And mountain-steeps and summits, whereunto
The vapours had receded, taking there
Their station under a cerulean sky.
Oh, 'twas an unimaginable sight!
Clouds, mists, streams, watery rocks and emerald turf,
Clouds of all tincture, rocks and sapphire sky,
Confused, commingled, mutually inflamed,
Molten together, and composing thus,
Each lost in each, that marvellous array
Of temple, palace, citadel, and huge
Fantastic pomp of structure without name,

In fleecy folds voluminous, enwrapped.
Right in the midst, where interspace appeared
Of open court, an object like a throne
Under a shining canopy of state
Stood fixed; and fixed resemblances were seen
To implements of ordinary use,
But vast in size, in substance glorified.

William Wordsworth

The Farmer's Bride

Three summers since I chose a maid,
        Too young maybe—but more's to do
        At harvest-time than bide and woo.
                        When us was wed she turned afraid
        Of love and me and all things human;
        Like the shut of a winter's day
        Her smile went out, and 'twadn't a woman—
                More like a little frightened fay.
                        One night, in the Fall, she runned away.

"Out 'mong the sheep, her be," they said,
'Should properly have been abed;
But sure enough she wadn't there
Lying awake with her wide brown stare.
So over seven-acre field and up-along across the down
        We chased her, flying like a hare
        Before our lanterns. To Church-Town
                All in a shiver and a scare
        We caught her, fetched her home at last
                And turned the key upon her, fast.

She does the work about the house
As well as most, but like a mouse:
        Happy enough to chat and play
        With birds and rabbits and such as they,
        So long as men-folk keep away.
"Not near, not near!" her eyes beseech
When one of us comes within reach.
        The women say that beasts in stall
        Look round like children at her call.
        I've hardly heard her speak at all.

Shy as a leveret, swift as he,
Straight and slight as a young larch tree,
Sweet as the first wild violets, she,
To her wild self. But what to me?

The short days shorten and the oaks are brown,
 The blue smoke rises to the low grey sky,
One leaf in the still air falls slowly down,
 A magpie's spotted feathers lie
On the black earth spread white with rime,
The berries redden up to Christmas-time.
 What's Christmas-time without there be
 Some other in the house than we!

 She sleeps up in the attic there
 Alone, poor maid. 'Tis but a stair
Betwixt us. Oh! my God! the down,
 The soft young down of her, the brown,
The brown of her—her eyes, her hair, her hair!

Charlotte Mew

The Fiddler of Dooney

When I play on my fiddle in Dooney,
Folk dance like a wave of the sea;
My cousin is priest in Kilvarnet,
My brother in Moharabuiee.

I passed my brother and cousin:
They read in their books of prayer;
I read in my book of songs
I bought at the Sligo fair.

When we come at the end of time,
To Peter sitting in state,
He will smile on the three old spirits,
But call me first through the gate;

For the good are always the merry,
Save by an evil chance,
And the merry love the fiddle
And the merry love to dance:

And when the folk there spy me,
They will all come up to me,
With 'Here is the fiddler of Dooney!'
And dance like a wave of the sea.

W. B. Yeats

The First Century

28. Your Enjoyment of the World is never right, till evry Morning you awake in Heaven: see your self in your fathers Palace: and look upon the Skies and the Earth and the Air, as Celestial Joys: having such a Reverend Esteem of all, as if you are among the Angels. The Bride of a Monarch, in her Husbands Chamber, hath no such Causes of Delight as you.

29. You never Enjoy the World aright, till the Sea it self floweth in your Veins, till you are Clothed with the Heavens, and Crowned with the Stars: and Perceiv your self to be the Sole Heir of the whole World: and more then so, becaus Men are in it who are evry one Sole Heirs, as well as you. Till you can Sing and Rejoyce and Delight in GOD, as Misers do in Gold, and Kings in Scepters, you never Enjoy the World.

30. Till your Spirit filleth the whole World, and the Stars are your Jewels, till you are as Familiar with the Ways of God in all Ages as with your Walk and Table: till you are intimatly Acquainted with that Shady Nothing out of which the World was made: till you lov Men so as to Desire their Happiness, with a Thirst equal to the zeal of your own: till you Delight in GOD for being Good to all: you never Enjoy the World. Till you more feel it than your Privat Estate, and are more present in the Hemisphere, Considering the Glories and the Beauties there, then in your own Hous. Till you remember how lately you were made, and how wonderfull it was when you came into it: and more rejoyce in the Palace of your Glory, then if it had been made but to Day Morning.

Thomas Traherne

Such joyous optimism!

The Jura

It is a spot which has all the solemnity, with none of the savageness, of the Alps; where there is a sense of a great power beginning to be manifested in the earth, and of a deep and majestic concord in the rise of the long low lines of piny hills; the first utterance of those mighty mountain symphonies, soon to be more loudly lifted and wildly broken along the battlements of the Alps. But their strength is as yet restrained; and the far reaching ridges of pastoral mountains succeed each other, like the long and sighing swell which moves over quiet waters from some far-off stormy sea. And there is a deep tenderness pervading that vast monotony. The destructive forces and the stern expression of the central ranges are alike withdrawn. No frost-ploughed, dust-encumbered paths of ancient glacier fret the soft Jura pastures; no splintered heaps of ruin break the fair ranks of her forest; no pale, defiled, or furious rivers send their rude and changeful ways among her rocks. Patiently, eddy by eddy, the clear green streams wind along their well-known beds; and under the dark quietness of the undisturbed pines, there spring up, year by year, such company of joyful flowers as I know not the like of among all the blessings of the earth. It was spring time, too; and all were coming forth in clusters crowded for very love; there was room enough for all, but they crushed their leaves into all manner of strange shapes only to be nearer each other. There was the wood anemone, star after star, closing every now and then into nebulae; and there was the oxalis, troop by troop, like virginal processions of the Mois de Marie, the dark vertical clefts in the limestone choked up with them as with heavy snow, and touched with ivy on the edges—ivy as light and lovely as the vine; and, ever and anon, a blue gush of violets, and cowslip bells in sunny places; and in the more open ground, the vetch, and comfrey, and mezereon, and the small sapphire buds of the Polygala Alpina, and the wild strawberry, just a blossom or two, all showered amidst the golden softness of deep, warm, amber-coloured moss.

John Ruskin, The Seven Lamps of Architecture *(1865)*

The Last Duke of Leeds

Sir d'Arcy Godolphin Osborne, British diplomatic envoy to the Vatican in 1936-47, was for the final eight months of his life, which he spent dozing, the twelfth and last Duke of Leeds, Marquis of Carmarthen, and Earl of Danby. I have felt tender sympathy for him since reading an entry in his diary: 'I am nothing but a pencilled marginal note in the Book of Life. I am not in the main text at all.' Self-effacement, when it is discreet and not an affectation, is a vanquishing attraction. Owen Chadwick, Regius Professor of Modern History at Cambridge, who was the Master of my college and taught me with filigree delicacy, drew on Osborne's diaries when writing his study Britain and the Vatican during the Second World War *(1986). The book includes this immaculate pen-portrait of the envoy to Popes Pius XI and XII:*

In February 1936 the new British Minister, d'Arcy Godolphin Osborne, arrived in Rome. He lived in a pleasant house with fair views at 36 Via Mercadante. He was unmarried, tall, and slim. His hair had receded, leaving a highbrow dome, and this made the face interesting and intelligent rather than handsome, indeed at times he could look comic. He had a bubbling gaiety, and was indefinably the grand seigneur in the best sense, with the simplest of manners, perfect but not too perfect courtesy and without the slightest trace of condescension. Rougher men sometimes criticized him for being formal, or overcorrect, or too tidy. He was liable to a little hypochondria. He was offended by noise, even by too loud laughter. But he was charming, and infinitely considerate. He had little money and suffered from extravagant tastes. He found it hard to resist works of art of doubtful authenticity. He liked his clothes, and wine, and whisky, and furniture, and silver, to be exactly what they ought to be. Some people thought him inclined to fuss about such outward things. He had aesthetic tastes, but was not critical in his judgments of art. He read a lot, but not with any academic judgment. He spoke French easily, and Italian, and had a wide knowledge of French literature.

The British Minister to the Holy See must be a Protestant, lest he suffer from a conflict of loyalties. Osborne was more than a mere conformist. He was wont to lift up a prayer at bed-time. If it became his duty to go to a papal mass, he could be (though he was not always) moved in soul. Once when he set out for Rome at a time when the journey was dangerous, he took the trouble to receive the sacrament in the Cornish parish church near the airfield from which he was to take off. But, at least in this stage of his life, he seldom appeared in church unless it were his duty. His mind sat loose to the orthodoxies.

He first visited Italy in 1900, but only fell in love with the country and its people during 1909-13 when he served as a junior in the diplomatic service under Lord Rennell. He looked back upon Rennell as the man who opened his eyes to the stature of Italy. When the First World War broke out he was in the embassy at Washington under Cecil Spring Rice. He had a short spell at The Hague; was in London 1920-28; then went for a short time to be counsellor in Lisbon; was back in Rome 1929-31; and then was minister at the embassy in Washington, from which he was summoned to be the British Minister to the Holy See.

His affection for the Italian people was a merit. And unlike most Englishmen of the moment, he had an unusual aspect in his liking for the Italians. He preferred them rather than the emperor Haile Selassie to govern Abyssinia. Haile Selassie could not stop the slave trade; the Italians could. But in that epoch of the British government's policy Osborne could not say this aloud.

His dressing-gown was of camel's hair, and he wore a George IV sovereign on his key-chain. He hated hats, especially the black hats affected by Anthony Eden and called by the name of that statesman. He hated wearing uniform and felt like a page-boy when correctly dressed as an ambassador. He refused ever to wear waistcoats. He liked pigskin, and caviare, and oysters, and Sheraton furniture, and expensive footwear. He disliked women who wore trousers. He had a touch of the introspective. People who saw him out for a solitary walk could fancy him rapt in deep thought. Certainly he was amusedly self-critical. He was amused to have his fortune told, and was interested in telepathy, and quarter-hoped that astrology might have something in it. He would have liked to believe in witches and the god Pan, though he confessed that the Vatican was not the likeliest place to see a witch sail by on a broomstick. With only a half-sceptical smile he wore a charm against cosmic rays.

He was a friend of the Duke and Duchess of York, soon to be King George VI and Queen Elizabeth. And generally he was a monarchist. He believed that Europe was better provided with constitutional government when kings sat upon their thrones. He mildly hankered after the restoration of a sovereign in France, and Spain, and Austria. He thought democracy only to work if it continually grew an aristocracy by successive accretions. He liked Americans very much, but was not sure that it was good for the North to have won the American Civil War. Slavery went, that was good, but there went with it an aristocracy with its spirit of chivalry. He was talented as an artist in water-colours. Children found him an unforgettable playmate.

Owen Chadwick

The Mudtower
(Tayport, Fife, 1 January 1975)

And again, without snow, a new year.
As for fifty years, thousands of years, the air
returns the child-blue rage of the river.
Six swans rise aloud from the estuary,
ferrying tremendous souls to the pond by the playground.
    They're coming for me! No. I'm part of the scenery.
They fly low, taking no interest in migratory ladies.

The stone town stumbles downhill to untidy mudflats—
high square houses shivering in windows, the street of shops,
the church and clocktower, school, the four worn pubs
artfully placed between dry rows of cottages.
Then council flats, fire station, rusty gasometer,
timber-yard baying its clean smell of pinewood;
grass, swings, mud ... the wilted estuary.

You could say that the winter's asleep in the harbour's arm.
Two sloops with their heads on their backs
            are sleeping there peacefully.
Far out in the tide's slum, in the arm of the sand-spit,
the mudtower wades in the giving and taking water.

Its uses—if it ever had uses—have been abandoned.
The low door's a mouth. Slit eyes stab the pinnacle.
Its lovethrust is made up from the mud it seems to be made of.
Surely it's alive and hibernating, Pictish or animal.
The seabirds can hear it breathing in its skin or shrine.
How these lighthouses, airing their bones on the coast,
hate the mudtower. They hold their bright messages aloft
like saints bearing scriptures.

As the water withdraws, the mudtower steps out on the land.
Watch the fierce, driven, hot-looking
Scuttlings of redshanks, the beaks of the oystercatchers.
Struggle and panic. Struggle and panic.
Mud's rituals resume. The priest-gulls flap to the kill.
Now high flocks of sandpipers, wings made of sunlight,
Flicker as snow flickers, blown from these inland hills.

Anne Stevenson

The Pavement Artist

The physical and nervous health of the barrister Herbert ('Beb') Asquith was wrecked by his military experiences in the Great War. He wrote this poem about an artist whom he knew to have enlisted in the army in 1914, and who did not return to his usual place on the pavement after the Armistice.

Before half-seeing eyes and hurrying feet
Five years ago in daily sacrifice
He laid the willows and the meadow-sweet:
Now he is gone, and all his sunlit skies
Are with the dust that floats along the street.
All vanished are the low-hushed tropic vales;
The glinting kingfisher; the lions' den;
And Nelson with his powder-blackened men
Gliding to action under tattered sails;
And near to these the wide Pacific calm,
And mirrored islands, where the tilted moon
Had left her trellis on the dark lagoon,
And sheathed in silver mail the tufted palm;
And divers groping on black ocean floors;
Deep-sunken ribs of wreck, where rusted doors
Are clamped on hidden gold, and sightless things
That flicker through the deep, where bubbles race
Up to the green light of the sun's embrace
And burst beneath the seagull's dipping wings.
And here was sunlight tossed upon the spray,
And coral pillars from the deep-sea bed
Gashing the crested surf in gleams of red;
And elephants with lordly gait a-sway,
Rocking their loads along dark forest ways;
The moth poised on the lily, and the pale
Diffusèd starlight on the nightingale,

Half-shadowed by the leaf from heaven's gaze.
And here the flying squirrel left the trees
To take his arrowy highroad through the sky;
Here armadillos walked, and peccaries,
And other creatures, stranger far than these,
But not more strange than you, who travelled by!
Great things and little from the undying Mind,
Toys fashioned in the morning of the earth,
Imagined by the gods, and brought to birth
For childhood in themselves or in mankind.
Artist, to some far garden are you gone
To find the great originals of these,
Under the streamers of the western sun,
Immortal butterflies, unfading trees!

Herbert Asquith

The Pike

From shadows of rich oaks outpeer
The moss-green bastions of the weir,
Where the quick dipper forages
In elver-peopled crevices.
And a small runlet trickling down the sluice
Gossamer music tires not to unloose.

Else round the broad pool's hush
Nothing stirs.
Unless sometime a straggling heifer crush
Through the thronged spinny whence the pheasant whirs;
Or martins in a flash
Come with wild mirth to dip their magical wings,
While in the shallow some doomed bulrush swings
At whose hid root the diver vole's teeth gnash.

And nigh this toppling reed, still as the dead
The great pike lies, the murderous patriarch,
Watching the waterpit shelving and dark
Where through the plash his lithe bright vassals thread.

The rose-finned roach and bluish bream
And staring ruffe steal up the stream
Hard by their glutted tyrant, now
Still as a sunken bough.

He on the sandbank lies,
Sunning himself long hours
With stony gorgon eyes:
Westward the hot sun lowers.

Sudden the grey pike changes, and quivering poises for slaughter;
   Intense terror wakens around him, the shoals scud awry, but there
       chances
     A chub unsuspecting; the prowling fins quicken, in fury he
       lances;
And the miller that opens the hatch stands amazed at the whirl
     in the water.

Edmund Blunden

'The Purse-Seine' was written by Robinson Jeffers in 1935 as part of a poetic sequence. I delight in the other poems to which it was attached in conception, 'The Coast-Road', 'The Wind-Struck Music', and 'Blind Horses'.

The Purse-Seine

Our sardine fishermen work at night in the dark of the moon;
    daylight or moonlight
They could not tell where to spread the net, unable to see the
    phosphorescence of the shoals of fish.
They work northward from Monterey, coasting Santa Cruz; off
    New Year's Point or off Pigeon Point
The look-out man will see some lakes of milk-color light on the sea's
    night-purple; he points, and the helmsman
Turns the dark prow, the motor-boat circles the gleaming shoal and
    drifts out her seine-net. They close the circle
And purse the bottom of the net, then with great labor haul it in.

      I cannot tell you
How beautiful the scene is, and a little terrible, then, when the
    crowded fish
Know they are caught, and wildly beat from one wall to the other of
    their closing destiny the phosphorescent
Water to a pool of flame, each beautiful slender body sheeted with
    flame, like a live rocket
A comet's tail wake of clear yellow flame; while outside the narrowing
Floats and cordage of the net great sea-lions come up to watch,
    sighing in the dark; the vast walls of night
Stand erect to the stars.

      Lately I was looking from a night mountain-top
On a wide city, the colored splendor, galaxies of light: how could I
    help but recall the seine-net

Gathering the luminous fish? I cannot tell you how beautiful the
　　city appeared, and a little terrible.
I thought, We have geared the machines and locked all together into
　　interdependence; we have built the great cities; now
There is no escape. We have gathered vast populations incapable of
　　free survival, insulated
From the strong earth, each person in himself helpless, on all
　　dependent. The circle is closed, and the net
Is being hauled in. They hardly feel the cords drawing, yet they shine
　　already. The inevitable mass-disasters
Will not come in our time nor in our children's, but we and our
　　children
Must watch the net draw narrower, government take all powers—or
　　revolution, and the new government
Take more than all, add to kept bodies kept souls—or anarchy, the
　　mass-disasters.

　　　　　These things are Progress;
Do you marvel our verse is troubled or frowning, while it keeps its
　　reason? Or it lets go, lets the mood flow
In the manner of the recent young men into mere hysteria,
　　splintered gleams, crackled laughter. But they are quite wrong.
There is no reason for amazement: surely one always knew that
　　cultures decay, and life's end is death.

　　　　　　　　　　　　　　　　　Robinson Jeffers

The Rake's Apology

Darling, let me lay it at your feet,
blinking and soft, a helpless little wolf-cub
huddled inside a gingham picnic-basket
on a cold night, on your doorstep, the fog
a clean slate, no sign of the coming flurry,
the never-ending blizzard. Do not worry.
Though it may break things, let it be your dog.
Snowed in, you'll feed it steak tartare and brisket,
its licked-clean bowl the colour of false love,
of the ice outside the window, of its teeth.

Tristram Fane Saunders

The Sun Rising

Busy old fool, unruly Sun,
   Why dost thou thus,
Through windows, and through curtains call on us?
Must to thy motions lovers' seasons run?
   Saucy pedantic wretch, go chide
   Late school boys and sour prentices,
  Go tell Court-huntsmen, that the King will ride,
  Call country ants to harvest offices;
Love, all alike, no season knows, nor clime,
Nor hours, days, months, which are the rags of time.

   Thy beams, so reverend, and strong
   Why shouldst thou think?
I could eclipse and cloud them with a wink,
But that I would not lose her sight so long:
   If her eyes have not blinded thine,
   Look, and tomorrow late, tell me,
  Whether both th' Indias of spice and Mine
  Be where thou left'st them, or lie here with me.
Ask for those kings whom thou saw'st yesterday,
And thou shalt hear, all here in one bed lay.

   She is all states, and all Princes, I,
   Nothing else is.
Princes do but play us; compared to this,
All honour's mimic; All wealth alchemy;
   Thou, sun, art half as happy as we,
   In that the world's contracted thus.
  Thine age asks ease, and since thy duties be
  To warm the world, that's done in warming us.
Shine here to us, and thou art everywhere;
This bed thy centre is, these walls, thy sphere.

John Donne

The Third Century

2

All appeared New, and Strange at the first, inexpressibly rare, and Delightfull, and Beautifull. I was a little Stranger which at my Enterance into the World was Saluted and Surrounded with innumerable Joys. My Knowledg was Divine. I knew by Intuition those things which since my Apostasie, I Collected again, by the Highest Reason. My very Ignorance was Advantageous. I seemed as one Brought into the Estate of Innocence. All Things were Spotles and Pure and Glorious: yea, and infinitly mine, and Joyfull and Precious. I Knew not that there were any Sins, or Complaints, or Laws. I Dreamed not of Poverties Contentions or Vices. All Tears and Quarrels, were hidden from mine Eys. Evry Thing was at Rest, Free, and Immortal. I Knew Nothing of Sickness or Death, or Exaction, in the Absence of these I was Entertained like an Angel with the Works of GOD in their Splendor and Glory; I saw all in the Peace of Eden; Heaven and Earth did sing my Creators Praises and could not make more Melody to Adam, than to me. All Time was Eternity, and a Perpetual Sabbath. Is it not Strange, that an Infant should be Heir of the World, and see those Mysteries which the Books of the Learned never unfold?

3

The Corn was Orient and Immortal Wheat, which never should be reaped, nor was ever sown. I thought it had stood from everlasting to everlasting. The Dust and Stones of the Street were as Precious as GOLD. The Gates were at first the End of the World, the Green Trees when I saw them first through one of the Gates Transported and Ravished me; their Sweetnes and unusual Beauty made my Heart to leap, and almost mad with Extasie, they were such strange and Wonderfull Thing: The Men! O what Venerable and Reverend Creatures did the Aged seem! Immortal Cherubims! And yong

Men Glittering and Sparkling Angels, and Maids strange Seraphick Pieces of Life and Beauty! Boys and Girles Tumbling in the Street, and Playing, were moving Jewels. I knew not that they were Born or should Die. But all things abided Eternaly as they were in their Proper Places. Eternity was Manifest in the Light of the Day, and som thing infinit Behind evry thing appeared: which talked with my Expectation and moved my Desire. The Citie seemed to stand in Eden, or to be Built in Heaven. The Streets were mine, the Temple was mine, the People were mine, their Clothes and Gold and Silver was mine, as much as their Sparkling Eys Fair Skins and ruddy faces. The Skies were mine, and so were the Sun and Moon and Stars, and all the World was mine, and I the only Spectator and Enjoyer of it. I knew no Churlish Proprieties, nor Bounds nor Divisions: but all Proprieties and Divisions were mine: all Treasures and the Possessors of them. So that with much adoe I was corrupted; and made to learn the Dirty Devices of this World. Which now I unlearn, and becom, as it were, a little Child again, that I may enter into the Kingdom of GOD.

Thomas Traherne

The Trees are Down

—and he cried with a loud voice:
Hurt not the earth, neither the sea, nor the trees—
(Revelation)

They are cutting down the great plane-trees at the end of the
gardens.
For days there has been the grate of the saw, the swish of the
branches as they fall,
The crash of trunks, the rustle of trodden leaves,
With the 'Whoops' and the 'Whoas,' the loud common talk,
the loud common laughs of the men, above it all.

I remember one evening of a long past Spring
Turning in at a gate, getting out of a cart, and finding a large
dead rat in the mud of the drive.
I remember thinking: alive or dead, a rat was a god-forsaken
thing,
But at least, in May, that even a rat should be alive.

The week's work here is as good as done. There is just one bough
On the roped bole, in the fine grey rain,
Green and high
And lonely against the sky.
(Down now!—)
And but for that,
If an old dead rat
Did once, for a moment, unmake the Spring, I might never have
thought of him again.

It is not for a moment the Spring is unmade to-day;
These were great trees, it was in them from root to stem:
When the men with the 'Whoops' and the 'Whoas' have carted
    the whole of the whispering loveliness away
Half the Spring, for me, will have gone with them.

It is going now, and my heart has been struck with the hearts of
    the planes;
Half my life it has beat with these, in the sun, in the rains,
     In the March wind, the May breeze,
In the great gales that came over to them across the roofs from
    the great seas.
      There was only a quiet rain when they were dying;
      They must have heard the sparrows flying,
And the small creeping creatures in the earth where they were
    lying—
      But I, all day, I heard an angel crying:
      'Hurt not the trees.'

Charlotte Mew

The World

I saw Eternity the other night,
Like a great ring of pure and endless light,
All calm, as it was bright;
And round beneath it, time in hours, days, years,
    Driv'n by the spheres
Like a vast shadow mov'd; in which the world
And all her train were hurl'd.
The doting lover in his quaintest strain
Did there complain;
Near him, his lute, his fancy, and his flights,
Wit's sour delights,
With gloves, and knots, the silly snares of pleasure,
Yet his dear treasure
All scatter'd lay, while he his eyes did pour
Upon a flow'r.

The darksome statesman hung with weights and woe,
Like a thick midnight-fog mov'd there so slow,
He did not stay, nor go;
Condemning thoughts (like sad eclipses) scowl
Upon his soul,
And clouds of crying witnesses without
Pursued him with one shout.
Yet digg'd the mole, and lest his ways be found,
Work'd under ground,
Where he did clutch his prey; but one did see
That policy;
Churches and altars fed him; perjuries
Were gnats and flies;
It rain'd about him blood and tears, but he
Drank them as free.

The fearful miser on a heap of rust
Sate pining all his life there, did scarce trust
His own hands with the dust,
Yet would not place one piece above, but lives
In fear of thieves;
Thousands there were as frantic as himself,
And hugg'd each one his pelf;
The downright epicure plac'd heav'n in sense,
And scorn'd pretence,
While others, slipp'd into a wide excess,
Said little less;
The weaker sort slight, trivial wares enslave,
Who think them brave;
And poor despised Truth sate counting by
Their victory.

Yet some, who all this while did weep and sing,
And sing, and weep, soar'd up into the ring;
But most would use no wing.
'O fools' (said I) 'thus to prefer dark night
Before true light,
To live in grots and caves, and hate the day
Because it shews the way,
The way, which from this dead and dark abode
Leads up to God,
A way where you might tread the sun, and be
More bright than he.'
But as I did their madness so discuss
One whisper'd thus,
'This ring the bride-groom did for none provide,
But for his bride.'

Henry Vaughan

Thompson's Lunch Room—Grand Central Station
Study in Whites

Wax-white—
Floor, ceiling, walls.
Ivory shadows
Over the pavement
Polished to cream surfaces
By constant sweeping.
The big room is coloured like the petals
Of a great magnolia,
And has a patina
Of flower bloom
Which makes it shine dimly
Under the electric lamps.
Chairs are ranged in rows
Like sepia seeds
Waiting fulfilment.
The chalk-white spot of a cook's cap
Moves unglossily against the vaguely bright wall—
Dull chalk-white striking the retina like a blow
Through the wavering uncertainty of steam.
Vitreous-white of glasses with green reflections,
Ice-green carboys, shifting—greener, bluer—with the jar of moving
    water.
Jagged green-white bowls of pressed glass
Rearing snow-peaks of chipped sugar
Above the lighthouse-shaped castors
Of grey pepper and grey-white salt.
Grey-white placards: "Oyster Stew, Cornbeef Hash, Frankfurters":
Marble slabs veined with words in meandering lines.
Dropping on the white counter like horn notes
Through a web of violins,
The flat yellow lights of oranges,

The cube-red splashes of apples,
In high plated *épergnes*.
The electric clock jerks every half-minute:
"Coming!—Past!"
"Three beef-steaks and a chicken-pie,"
Bawled through a slide while the clock jerks heavily.
A man carries a china mug of coffee to a distant chair.
Two rice puddings and a salmon salad
Are pushed over the counter;
The unfulfilled chairs open to receive them.
A spoon falls upon the floor with the impact of metal striking stone,
And the sound throws across the room
Sharp, invisible zigzags
Of silver.

Amy Lowell

Did this poem influence Auden, I wonder, when in 1949 he wrote his beatific vision 'In Shraffts'?

Thrush
(i.m. Ted Hughes)

Giant eye, a livid yellow and black-rimmed eye,
   furious and feral, met my own at eye height
inches away. It happened like this. A male thrush,
   a big one with obese breast and thick feathering
got caught in the holly hedge which we had planted
   oh thirty years gone. Seventeenth century Welsh
farmhouse plonked down on a hospitable plateau
   that interrupted the steep south-falling hillock,
no doubt through interglacial realignment
   ten or twelve thousand years old but an eyeblink
in the planet story. It welcomed nonetheless
   space for a dwelling, attendant barns and stables,
built on now, gentrified, yeomanified really,
   in the 1830s. The hill fell steep again
where a front lawn should be then swept gently away
   to the river Cain (cf. *cattle* not *fratricide*).
So you get to the house by a sunken drover's
   lane with a stone retaining-wall, a holly hedge
all over it. So—getting on now, lame, grumpy –
   I found myself eyeball to eyeball with a thrush
and man to man, him being formidably male
   and not at all frightened but furious to rage
at me and my holly, poor excuses for life.
   It was hard to get over that reptilian
eye, so livid and yellow, or that bad black look
   and something of the crocodile coiled within it,
the beak spiky like holly, the angry pounding
   of a mottled breast, the eye on a par with mine.
I leaned on the wall, poked with my standard-issue
   NHS lightweight crutch deep into the holly
for a parting of ways, just to liberate him

from so much anger and hostility, myself
from both of these and let me hobble home for tea.
    It worked. After so long, so entirely song-less
a scrabbling, my thrush plummets improbably free
to lumber into the sky like some miniature
jumbo jet taking off and elegant only
    with height accomplished. And so horrible for him.
He almost didn't make it, had almost fallen
    out of his painful prison, just in time to step
back into the sky milliseconds from rough ground,
    from earth or all we covet down here of freedom.
After a few clumsy feet his elevation
    pumped all the oxygen out of his mottled chest
and he flew so fast and so in an instant high
    that he looked tiny now and full of the rapture
of a fighter plane or Old Master depiction
of some soul leaving its body; leaving desire,
anger, frustration, appetite; and leaving me
    to waver and shuffle, try to get back to life,
get on with life or whatever was left of life;
    unable almost to breathe or turn home to slake
the ancient malevolence in that yellow eye.

Grey Gowrie

To a friend whose work has come to nothing

Now all the truth is out,
Be secret and take defeat
From any brazen throat,
For how can you compete,
Being honour bred, with one
Who were it proved he lies
Were neither shamed in his own
Nor in his neighbours' eyes;
Bred to a harder thing
Than Triumph, turn away
And like a laughing string
Whereon mad fingers play
Amid a place of stone,
Be secret and exult,
Because of all things known
That is most difficult.

W. B. Yeats

To the Same Purpose

To the same purpos: he, not long before
Brought home from Nurse, went to the door
To do som little thing
He must not do within,
With Wonder cries,
As in the Skies
He saw the Moon, *O yonder is the Moon,*
Newly com after me to Town,
That shin'd at Lugwardin but yesternight,
Where I enjoy'd the self-same sight.

As if it had ev'n twenty thousand faces,
It shines at once in many places;
To all the Earth so wide
God doth the Stars divide,
With so much Art
The Moon impart,
They serve us all; serve wholy ev'ry one
As if they served him alone.
While evry single Person hath such Store,
'Tis want of Sense that makes us poor.

Thomas Traherne

Two Evenings

It was the time of dusk when lorry-drivers,
Running from Durham north to sea-fog nights,
Think about sleep, and switch on long-beamed lights
And the engine's monotonous drumming for a moment dies;
The time when half-light draws a fading gleam
From railway tracks, and ugly, unloved lovers,
Settling alone in trains to silent meals,
Hear a quickening of the wheels,
And see their faces trickling through the steam,
On carriage windows colder than their eyes.
I climbed upstairs about that time of day
Watching the last light set,
Then through an echoing flat could not forget
How evening felt before you were away.

Alasdair Clayre

Two Friends

They were two friends, but very little like:
The one a hard, keen, literary mind,
As nimble as the serpent's quivering tongue,
Incisive, analytic, full of gibes,
Yet true and loyal in its narrow sphere,
Hating all mystery. To him the world
Seemed rounded off in perfect symmetry,
And all thoughts might be gauged. Five senses give
All that we know, and nothing lies beyond,
Though Fancy, Passion, Int'rest take those thoughts
And blend them into stately cloudy forms,
Baseless and fleeting soon. The stars to him
Were but an endless range of common earths;
And that strange voice which in the mind of man
Commands and awes was but an echo formed
By custom, prejudice, or ancient use;
And if at times, like music far and low,
In hours of pain or solitude or grief
Wild longings swept unbidden o'er his soul,
He deemed them but the signs of shattered nerves,
Or childish memories soon to be repressed
By rising reason. So he lived, and so
At length will die.
            With him there lived a friend,
Dear to his heart, born in a Southern land,
Where thought is steeped in passion, with a mind
Deep, vague, and lustrous, as a Spanish eye,
Floating in light of dreams. His ear was quick
To catch the finer melodies of life.
The wonder and the mystery that bound
Man's little segment of the truth of things
Filled him with awe; and as he looked within

He saw, or seemed to see, across the gloom
Dim broken lines that pointed to the sky,
And prints and characters of nobler source
Than sense can furnish—those deep-rooted hopes
Which grow and brighten with our better moods,
And pure ideals never here attained,
And craving needs which earth can never sate,
And love too fond for passing men to feel
If all were closed and ended in the tomb:
And chiefly that strange law that in a world
Of joys and pains a something higher rules—
Rules by acknowledged right, though often spurned.
The twilight visions of a noble soul
Were to him sacred, and the Spirit-forms
That, faint and feeble, seem to flicker there
Were more than phantoms or than earth-borne mists.
Above his head he saw the milky way,
Dim blending lights of countless distant worlds.

W. E. H. Lecky

John Masefield wrote this address to mark his investiture with an honorary degree at the University of Sheffield in June 1946.

Universities

There are few earthly things more splendid than a university.
In these days of broken frontiers and collapsing values,
when the dams are down and the floods are making misery,
when every ancient foothold has become something of a quagmire,
wherever a university stands, it stands and shines;
wherever it exists, the free minds of men, urged on to full and fair
     enquiry,
may still bring wisdom into human affairs.

There are few earthly things more beautiful than a university.
It is a place where those who hate ignorance may strive to know,
where those who perceive truth may strive to make others see;
where seekers and learners alike,
banded together in the search for knowledge,
will honour thought in all its finer ways,
will welcome thinkers in distress or in exile,
will uphold ever the dignity of thought and learning,
and will exact standards in these things.
They give to the young in their impressionable years,
the bond of a lofty purpose shared,
of a great corporate life whose links will not be loosed until they die.
They give young people that close companionship for which youth
     longs,
and that chance of the endless discussion of the themes which are
     endless,
without which youth would seem a waste of time.

There are few things more enduring than a university.
Religions may split into sect or heresy;

dynasties may perish or be supplanted,
but for century after century the university will continue,
and the stream of life will pass through it,
and the thinker and the seeker will be bound together
in the undying cause of bringing thought into the world.
To be a member of these great societies
must ever be a glad distinction.

John Masefield

Washing

Plasencia stands in the high valley of the river Jerte.

There are the usual narrow paved streets knotted about the hills, the usual Plaza and its arcades, the hundred little trades, the drab, soiled cafés, where the faded provincial people sit drinking beer or coffee, playing chess in little groups or sitting alone, large tawny moons of silence and digestion. Storks crackle their beaks above the roofs. The convent bells crack hours and hit prayers.

In the heat, all men and animals make for the sight of water. It is Monday, the great washing-day, and the cliffs, the rocks, the river banks for a mile about the town are white with drying linen. There are areas of sheets lying about so that you cannot get within twenty yards of the river without treading on them. All the women of Plasencia are washing sheets, night-gowns, and underclothes in the bubbling green Jerte, now lively as a field of lilies with the snow water of the mountains of Béjar. The water is combed over the weirs to the north of the town and so broadens into a wide sweep along a field smooth as an altar-cloth on which poplars are green candles, with the sunlight burning at their tops and running guttering down their sides. A grey donkey stands hee-hawing there with his tail recoiled like a thick serpent stiffening to dart. Two or three men wade mules across the river, where it is not more than three feet deep, on to a bank of shingle, and in that glaring bank stand as hot as flies, gathering baskets full of stones and emptying them into the panniers of the mules, driving them up again into the town where a school is being built. There is a breeze at this point where the valley has opened greenly between the barrancos and the shaking olive-braided hills. All day long horses and donkeys are watered in the stream.

Between the two bridges and even beyond them the town is encircled by washing. The women, with large straw hats over their heads, kneel by the river. Some merely fling their garment into the river and pull it out. The conscientious scrub on boards or between the fists, and a bluish veil of suds is drawn out by the fingers of the current and floats down stream, where the water becomes deep and olive. Again breaking into shallows, it is a talking, living passage of light over the pebbles, and the singing of the women is carried over it and mingles with the chatter, the pouring, the trilling, and swishing. Oick. Oick, oie-e-e-e-e, the pure whistle and the thin fife, until the sung words of the women are dark fish passing from light to light and merging into the hanging shadows of the ripples, disappearing as the water deepens for a rush under the middle arches of the old bridge, and thence, full of body and still, presses a course into the barrancos. The women of Plasencia call minor songs among the ripples, and their voices rise from the live throat of the stream, lark-like, water-mingling jubilee in the Arab minor. As the silt is worked off by the river as it laves the body of the land, it carries away the gritty voices of the women of Plasencia across Spain to the sea. Notes and voices like knocking pebbles, jingling like pence, voices of silver darkness. Songs like the stream drenching over the weirs or speaking among the sallying boulders, choruses that divide among sporadic rapids and turn about gaily in whirlpools, and dart off once more in the deep olive minor, and rise trilling again with laughter. Scrub and wring and shake your white things among the voices of the water, the voices of the sun, the mountains and their winds; plunge the arm into the reflections of a town that hangs upside down from its splindling shadow legs like marionettes; churches, houses, mills, and monasteries, cypresses and oranges, singing away to nothing. Each garment a song with a chime of laughter.

V. S. Pritchett, Marching Spain

Wish

I wish I could show you like waking Adam
A world of flower, of bird and tree
   Where each stream sang its name
Every beast printed its story:
There would be fields butterflies patterned
And there, jewel and dress, from a wood
Kingfishers would fly to your hand
   In words I remembered from childhood;
But the garden has to be made of rain
Across steel, brick, drooping coalsmoke:
   No easy beauty,
   Only the locked sea
   Pockmarked here in a dock,
And an asphalt pavement rainbow-flowered with oilstain.

Alasdair Clayre

Wonder

How like an Angel came I down!
　　How bright are all things here!
When first among his Works I did appear
　　O how their Glory me did crown!
The World resembled his *ETERNITY*,
　　　In which my Soul did walk;
　　And ev'ry Thing that I did see
　　　Did with me talk.

　　The Skies in their Magnificence,
　　　The lovly, lively Air,
Oh how divine, how soft, how sweet, how fair!
　　The Stars did entertain my Sense,
And all the Works of God, so bright and pure,
　　　So rich and great, did seem,
　　As if they ever must endure
　　　In my Esteem.

　　A Nativ Health and Innocence
　　　Within my Bones did grow,
And while my God did all his Glories show,
　　I felt a vigor in my Sense
That was all SPIRIT. I within did flow
　　　With Seas of Life, like Wine;
　　I nothing in the World did know
　　　But 'twas Divine.

Harsh rugged Objects were conceal'd,
    Oppressions, Tears, and Cries,
Sins, Griefs, Complaints, Dissentions, weeping eys
    Were hid, and only things reveal'd
Which heav'nly Spirits, and the Angels prize.
      The State of Innocence
    And Bliss, not Trades and Poverties,
        Did fill my Sense.

The streets seem'd pav'd with golden Stones,
    The Boys and Girls all mine,
To me how did their lovly faces shine!
    The Sons of men all Holy ones,
In Joy and Beauty, then appear'd to me;
      And evry Thing I found
While like an Angel I did see,
      Adorn'd the Ground.

Rich Diamond, and Pearl, and Gold
    In ev'ry place was seen;
Rare Splendors, Yellow, Blew, Red, White and Green,
    Mine Eys did evrywhere behold.
Great Wonders cloth'd with Glory did appear,
      Amazement was my Bliss,
    That and my Wealth was ev'ry where:
      No Joy to this!

Curs'd and devis'd proprieties,
     With Envy, Avarice
And Fraud, those Feinds that Spoyl even Paradice,
     Fled from the Splendor of mine Eys,
And so did Hedges, Ditches, Limits, Bounds,
     I dream'd not aught of those,
     But wander'd over all men's Grounds,
          And found Repose.

Proprieties themselves were mine,
     And Hedges Ornaments;
Walls, Boxes, Coffers, and their rich Contents
     Did not Divide my Joys, but all combine.
Clothes, Ribbons, Jewels, Laces, I esteem'd
     My Joys by others worn:
     For me they all to wear them seem'd
          When I was born.

Thomas Traherne

Acknowledgements

I thank Joshua Bennett for permission to reproduce his poem 'Owed to the Tardigrade'; Helen Chadwick for her permission to quote from the prose of her father Owen Chadwick; Tristram Fane Saunders for his agreement to my reproduction of 'The Rake's Apology' from *The Rake* (Poetry Business, 2022); Adelheid, Countess of Gowrie for permission to reproduce her husband's poems 'Gardener's Tale' and 'The Thrush'; Jennie Lubbock for her consent to my use of a passage from her uncle's memoir *Earlham*; Mary Hope for permission to reproduce her husband's poem *'Schlossbesuch'* from *Instead of a Poet, and other poems* (The Bodley Head, 1965); David Pryce-Jones for his consent to quote from the published journals of his father Alan Pryce-Jones, *Devoid of Shyness*, edited by John Byrne (Stone Trough Books, 2015); Celia Roberts, for permission to use two poems by her aunt Ruth Pitter; Martha Sprackland, for permission to reproduce her poem 'Dappled Things'; Blair Worden, literary executor of Lord Dacre of Glanton, for the extracts from Hugh Trevor-Roper's war journals; and Andrew Wynn Owen for permission to reproduce 'The Door' (from his collection *Multiverse*, 2018).

'Ten to Six' by Sara Berkeley is reprinted from her collection *The Last Cold Day* (Gallery Press, 2022). 'No Continuing City' and 'The Pike' by Edmund Blunden, from *The Poems of Edmund Blunden 1914-1930* (Cobden Sanderson, 1930), are reproduced by permission of David Higham Associates. The extract from *The Hotel* by Elizabeth Bowen is reproduced with permission of Curtis Brown Group Ltd., London, on behalf of the literary executors of the estate of Elizabeth Bowen. Peters, Fraser & Dunlop, representing the literary estate of Alasdair Clayre, have permitted me to reproduce his poems 'Melanie Klein's Theory' and 'Wish'. I thank the Literary Trustees of

Walter de la Mare and The Society of Authors as their representative for permission to reproduce 'Idleness' and 'Of a Son'. The sonnet 'Mechanic repairing a motor-cycle' is reproduced by courtesy of the Estate of Geoffrey Faber. 'After Adomnán' by Tom French is reproduced from his collection *The Sea Field* (Gallery Press, 2020); and his poems 'Breeches Church, Pollagh' and 'Commission' are from *Company* (Gallery Press, 2022). 'Some Waves' and 'The Lesson' are from Kevin Graham, *The Look-Out Post* (Gallery Press, 2023). 'The Purse-Seine' by Robinson Jeffers is reprinted from his *Collected Poetry*, volume 2, edited by Tim Hunt (Stanford University Press, 1994), by permission of the editor and publisher. 'Country Sounds' and 'In Such Slow Sweetness' by Elizabeth Jennings, from *The Collected Poems* (Carcanet Press) are reproduced by permission of David Higham Associates. The poems by Patrick Kavanagh are reprinted from his Collected Poems, edited by Antoinette Quinn (Allen Lane, 2004), by kind permission of the Trustees of the Estate of the late Katherine B. Kavanagh, through the Jonathan Williams Literary Agency.

'Penshurst Place' by Derek Mahon is from *The Poems (1961-2020)* (Gallery Press, 2021). John Masefield's address 'Universities' and extracts from his poem 'August 1914' are made by courtesy of the Society of Authors as the literary representative of the Estate of John Masefield. The poem 'Love' by Eiléan Ni Chuilleanáin is from her *Collected Poems* (Gallery Press, 2020). Jonathan Price's poem 'The Camp' is reproduced by permission of his son Tim Price from his collection *Everything Must Go* (Secker & Warburg, 1985). Peters, Fraser & Dunlop, representing the literary estate of Sir V. S. Pritchett, have permitted me to quote paragraphs from *Marching Spain*. The poems by Sally Purcell are reprinted by permission of Carcanet from her *Collected Poems*, edited by Peter Jay (Anvil Press Poetry, 2002). 'Childhood' and '1945' by Herbert Read, from *Collected Poems* (Faber & Faber, 1946); reproduced by permission of David Higham Associates. 'A Painting by Winifred Nicholson' and 'Card-table' by Kathleen Raine are reproduced by permission of Faber & Faber. The poems by Anne Ridler are reprinted by permission of Carcanet from her *Collected Poems* (Carcanet, 1994). Two poems by E. J. Scovell are reprinted with the permission of Carcanet. 'Dappled Things' from *Citadel* by Martha Sprackland (Pavilion Poetry, Liverpool University Press, 2020), was first published by Caught by the River. The poems by Anne Stevenson are from her *Collected Poems* (Bloodaxe Books, 2023).

Strenuous efforts have been made by the compiler to contact copyright holders. They are asked to contact him if any rights have been overlooked.

Index of authors